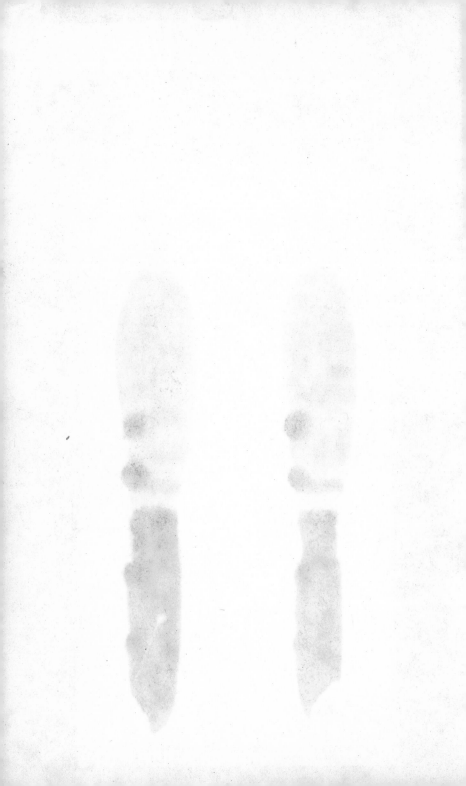

Mourning Glory

MOURNING GLORY

The Making of a Marine

By

David J. Regan

THE DEVIN-ADAIR COMPANY
Old Greenwich, Connecticut

To Lisa McCauley, my friend

For information address The Devin-Adair Company, 143 Sound Beach Avenue, Old Greenwich, Connecticut 06870.

Library of Congress Catalog Card Number: 80-67134
ISBN: 0-8159-6218-5

Manufactured in the United States of America

PROLOGUE

I began preparing for war on my third birthday. It was on that day that my uncle from Los Angeles came to visit and tell us of his exciting adventures as a world traveler. I distinctly remember his khaki-colored African safari shirt with the loops on the shoulders and his broad arms full of gifts for the children, especially me.

I also recall clearly my reaction to the present that Uncle Louis handed me with a flourish. I felt a mixture of fear and excitement as I examined the white plastic-handled set of matching cap pistols and the finely tooled leather holsters. For some reason, either learned or instinctive, the guns were not toys to me. They were too heavy and well balanced, too precisely machined, to be playthings. For the hour or so that the pistols were "brand-new" they were real guns. It was my first taste of the power that comes from being well armed. I make no case for the madness or sanity of the feeling but I invite you to put a loaded pistol in your pocket or purse and go out for a short walk. I assure you that it will feel quite different from your ordinary evening constitutional.

From these small beginnings my education in the proper way for a man to conduct himself grew in direct ratio to the amount of television I watched. From the innocent Mighty Mouse who swooped out of the sky every Saturday morning and laid his opponents to waste with his super charged fists to the more sophisticated weaponry of the Texas Rangers, Matt Dillon, Sgt. Joe Friday, and the ever-present John Wayne, I learned the difference between good guys and bad guys, courage and cowardice, and male and female. It was quite simple and after the scenario was repeated several thousand times I knew with complete certainty that women were noble but weak, that the bad guys existed in order to be killed by the good guys, and that courage was a sort of armor that ensured the good guy's survival.

With an education in the facts of life thoroughly imbedded in my mind, it was only the next logical step when Camelot swept onto the national scene. I was in the eighth grade at a Catholic school, just learning not to French kiss, when Jack and Jackie were installed as the most colorful and inspiring First Family in history.

We had a TV in the classroom as Jack instructed us in his famous voice to "ask not what your country can do for you—ask what you can do for your country." We saw the first trickling of news from Indo-China on TV after the President sent his ultra-macho Green Berets there. The tube recorded the shattering events of November 22, 1963 and the landslide reelection of Jack's sidekick, Lyndon.

Since the basic values of manhood were part and parcel of my thinking it was a natural and easy decision to join the Marines shortly after my seventeenth birthday. Like the majority of the boys at that time I was ready for an adventure, and the excellent public relations campaign the Corps conducted sealed my choice.

What the Marines knew and I didn't was that the symbols of manliness my generation grew up with were illusions. Watching John Wayne wipe out machine gun nests was sufficient indoctrination to get someone to volunteer for the Marines but it fell far short of the level of motivation required to actually confront real bullets, real blood and real fear.

The mission that the Marines had to accomplish with us was basically twofold. First, they had to destroy utterly our notion that we were unique individuals capable of and desiring self-determination. This task, if completed successfully, would transform a number of individuals into a completely obedient group. Second, they had to tap, bring to the surface, and reinforce a desire that exists deep in the minds of all men, the desire to look boldly into the face of death and conquer the gut-deep panic that results.

The hoped-for end result of marine training is an utterly obedient soldier who desires above all things the glory of successful combat.

However, no amount of training or brainwashing can prepare a man fully for the reality of war. In order to reach the state of brutal savagery and hatred that combat calls for, one must, of necessity, first live through a few skirmishes.

The final and macabre joke is that Chance is the major factor in war's equation. Skill, cunning, lack of remorse, and caution all play a part in the outcome of battle, but without Lady Luck to pave the way one does not return home alive. The absolute cruelty of war is the inescapable fact that simple luck, like a haphazard roll of the dice, is the decider of one's fate. The deep and inexpressible frustration that we felt each time fate claimed one of our friends was the most intense emotion that we experienced in Vietnam. If someone made a hero gesture and lost, it was understandable. If someone was daydreaming instead of watching for booby traps and got nailed it was explainable. But when someone caught a tiny piece of shrapnel in the spinal cord, we could not see a logical explanation for it. Why not a quarter inch to the right or left? A minor nick becoming a lifetime in a wheelchair could not be accepted.

There were a few people who laid claim to the glory they sought. There were men in the Marines who had a limitless appetite for the machismo and power that battle provides. The rest of us found weariness, degradation and premature middle age. We learned, fifty years before our natural time, how to mourn for our peers. We pursued death in order to face and overcome it but, like millions who have gone before us, we came to understand that all of man's brave talk and all of his lust for life mean nothing when death erases him.

A few found glory but all of us learned to mourn. This story is factual. Having no desire to reopen freshly healed wounds I have changed all names.

—D.R.

I wish to thank:

Jan McCauley. She calmly weathered my storms and continues to give me encouragement every day.

L. Ron Hubbard. His mental techniques cleared the trauma of Vietnam from my mind, after the "experts" had failed.

Lt. Don Brown, USMC retired. He said the right thing at the right time.

CHAPTER ONE

...Alice started to her feet, for it flashed across her mind that she had never before seen a rabbit with either a waistcoat pocket, or a watch to take out of it, and, burning with curiosity, she ran across the field after it, and was just in time to see it pop down a large rabbit hole under the hedge.

In another moment down went Alice after it, never once considering how in the world she was to get out again.

I was deliberately aloof at the airport in San Diego as I slowly dragged on my Lucky Strike and waited for the beginning of what would prove to be the most mind-boggling journey of my young life.

The group that I was traveling with consisted of twenty young men aged seventeen to twenty-three whose backgrounds were as different as the seasons in our home state of Minnesota.

I watched with mild disdain as the majority of the boys bantered and milled around. The hick-town enthusiasm of the group was disturbing the cosmopolitan sophistication that I was displaying for the benefit of the onlookers.

In due time a green school bus with yellow markings pulled up to the curb in front of the sidewalk where we were loosely assembled and a Marine Sergeant stepped coolly off. The letters on the side of the bus read "United States Marine Corps Recruit Depot."

The Sergeant was immaculately attired in the famous blue uniform of the Corps. He had multicolored campaign ribbons and silver shooting medals on his chest, bright yellow longevity stripes on the forearm, Sgt.'s insignia on the bicep, and the beloved symbol of the Corps: the eagle, globe, and anchor, gleaming in brilliant gold on his collar. This display, set off by the red piping on the coat and red stripe down the leg of the trousers, was complemented very nicely by the man that the uniform contained. His head was shaved bald at the sides and was cropped in a military flattop above. The deeply tanned and chiseled features of his face conveyed an expression of strength and discipline.

With a sparkle in his eyes and a welcoming nod he said "OK men, just line up here and I'll get you checked off on the roster and situated in the bus. I'd like you to answer up when I call your name. Just say 'here.'"

We sauntered onto the bus, making wisecracks and laughing loudly. I made my way to a vacant seat, slouched down, and waited for the remainder of the group to board.

When the last man entered the doorway and found a seat the Sgt. sprang nimbly up the steps and motioned for the driver to close the doors. Turning to face us our host said "Shut the windows now, please."

After several minutes and much commotion the windows were closed, the outside world was effectively sealed away, and all that was heard was the excited murmur of young men on an adventure into the unknown.

The bus began moving at a signal from the still standing Sgt. and we were on our way.

"Shut your goddam fucking slimy mouths you scumbag filth!" The shout was an icy, piercing, utterly commanding shock. Every man on the bus, regardless of size or background, was instantly seized by fear. The command hung in the air, suspended by the very incredibility of it.

"You turds keep your eyes to the front! Burn a hole in the head in front of you! If I hear one peep, if I see one movement before we reach our destination—I'm gonna crush your fuckin' brain!"

On that note we were welcomed to our home of the next eleven weeks.

2

I sat motionless on the bus as we rolled through the streets of San Diego. The only thing that I was aware of during the ride was the head in front of me, flickering streaks of light from the street lamps, muffled and unidentifiable noises leaking in through the cracks in our vehicle's shell, and the hard knot of apprehension in my guts.

Although the tension created by thirty men wishing to remove themselves and being unable to do so was nearly unbearable, nobody tested the Sgt.'s promise of blood and mayhem by moving. Therefore, we survived the bus ride to MCRD.

As we passed through the gates at the base my first thought was how similar the place was to what I had always pictured as prison. My second thought was escape. I risked a quick glance at the uniformed guards and saw "robots" instead of the glamorous macho image that I had been expecting. I had three years, eleven months, twenty-nine days, twenty-three and three-quarters hours left to serve of my four-year enlistment and I was already wishing I was out.

The bus rolled to a halt in front of a building that was brightly lit and seemed to be a combination of office building and barracks. Our reception party was about to begin.

"Listen up swine! Listen up real close and impress what I'm about to tell you on your fuckin' brains cause you won't get a second chance. Your memory might belong to your mama and your soul might belong to God but as of right now your fuckin' ass belongs to the Marine Corps! Whether you like it or don't like it, you're gonna do just exactly what the fuck you're told to do. If for some reason you choose to follow your own fucked-up civilian ways, well, God and mama can have their part of you cause there ain't gonna be nothing else left! Bear strongly in your fuckin' minds that there are people here who want to KILL you and if you give them a chance it's your own goddam problem."

The Sergeant's voice then took on the rhythm and cadence of a machine gun chant. "When I give you the word...you will disembark from this vee-hicle in single file. You will begin with the right front seat and continue toward the rear until the right side is completely empty. The left side will then do the same.

3

When you step off this vee-hicle you will run as fast as you can to the Corporal who is waiting for you in front of the hatch leading into the building. You will fall in on the yellow footprints, eyes straight ahead and thumbs along the seams of the trousers. You will not scratch, fidget, shuffle, or look to either port or starboard. You will be perfectly silent and if possible you will not breathe. Now do it, girls, move! Quickly! Quickly! Get the fuck off this bus! MOVE! MOVE! MOVE!"

Somehow the bus was unloaded without injury and with the screams of the Sgt. luring us along we managed to start lining up on the yellow footprints.

We were now under the command of another marine; this one taller, thinner, and meaner looking than the last. The Corporal was screaming and cursing us, enraged by the slowness that he perceived. He sharply slapped one of the boys from St. Paul who made the mistake of glancing away from the head in front of him.

I thought there must be a mistake when I got into the formation and took my spot on a vacant set of painted footprints. The first pair that I stepped on were so close to the man in front that we were touching, so I stepped back to the next set of footprints which were a more normal distance away from the next recruit.

The Corporal was ranting and bellowing, "Close it up, you goddam fucking people, you fucking scum! Fill in those footprints before I start killing a few of you worthless maggots!"

I was not about to argue with the man so I stepped up to the first prints I had picked out and hoped I was right. The footprints I had just vacated were quickly filled in by another man.

"This can't be right! Is this right?! What's going on here?" my thoughts were beginning to jam. My nose was about two inches from the person in front of me and my groin was pressed tightly against his ass. The person in back was smashed against me also. I was sandwiched between two sweaty men, the Corporal was still screaming, and I was now on the verge of panic.

"That's it, ladies, asshole to bellybutton, squeeze up there and make that turd in front of you smile! You're gonna be together for a long time and I want you to get acquainted with your neighbors."

4

I peeked over at the Corporal and he was sporting a wide grin, enjoying our discomfort and his role as the perpetrator of it.

He was finally satisfied with our formation and introduced himself. "My name is Corporal James and I got you mother-fuckers by the balls. The first thing we do here is cut your goddam hair off and make you look like men rather than faggots. You will be absolutely silent at all times and will stand at attention whenever you are not carrying out an order." He paused to survey us. "The first squad will doubletime through that hatch and take a seat in the barber's chair. There will be a turd standing at attention in front of the chair ready to move in as soon as the man in front of you is finished. You have permission to speak to the barber if you have sores on your head and wish to tell him so. The first word out of your mouth is always sir. When your haircut is completed you will be given directions regarding the next thing you are to do. First squad move out!"

As the squad headed toward the door they were met by two more marines. The two new ones were wearing green fatigues and smokey bear hats and were of the same approximate physical makeup as Corporal James. They were definitely of the same angry disposition.

"Move, Move, Move! Get in step people! What the fuck you waiting for asshole, an invitation? Get up in that fucking chair screwhead! Next! Quickly! Let's go! You don't like that boy? Get in there, nigger! Second squad, move out! Go!"

It was my turn. Hair was flying in every possible direction. Cursing, ranting men were bullying everybody in sight. The noise and confusion were overwhelming and all I wanted was to survive. SLAP! *Goddam you turd!* You looked at me! Keep your fucking ass at attention or die!"

I climbed into the chair and looked straight ahead. With no preliminaries, no sheet to catch the hair, and with a coldness born of hatred the barber slashed the hair off my head in half a dozen long rough strokes. Another half dozen smaller snips and I was as bald as the day I was born. I was also as helpless and confused.

"Get the fuck out of my chair!" the barber screamed in

my ear. I scrambled down and ran into the next room leaving a large hunk of my identity on the barbershop floor.

The room I had entered was large and barren with the exception of a long, chest-high table running the entire length of one wall. Behind the table were shelves stocked with clothing and gear. About every ten feet a marine was stationed behind the table and had the job of giving out the item he was in charge of to the recruits passing through. The first marine threw a large bag at me. He said, "This is a mattress cover, a goddam fartsack. Hold it open in front of you as you go down the line. Side-step and keep your eyes straight to the front!"

The next marine I stopped in front of shouted, "Shoe size!" "Sir, size eight" I squeaked back. The marine stooped to a bin marked eight, picked up a pair of black shoes and threw them into my open fartsack. This was followed by two pairs of combat boots.

I was swept along in that manner until I had received the full allotment of gear. I managed to avoid any type of confrontation by shouting the various sizes loud and clear and keeping my body at a position of rigid attention.

The combination of recruits crying out their sizes, the supply men yelling at the recruits, and the drill instructors shouting their favorite litany of courses destroyed any idea of regrouping and collecting my wits. All of the other privates were in the same condition and the net result was that terror and chaos reigned supreme. Any thought of forming a mental defense against the onslaught was smashed away before it could even begin to take hold.

I followed the recruit ahead of me into a hallway outside of the supply room and joined the formation that was there. We crushed in and stood holding our sacks, now heavily laden with gear, six inches off the floor.

I managed to place myself in the middle of the group—a position that seemed like a natural hiding place. There was much less noise in the hallway and in the relative calm I had my first chance to assess the situation which confronted us.

This was not what I had been expecting at all. I had imagined boot camp to be a fort of some kind where we would camp out in the woods and play marine. I was told it would be "tough" and would make a man out of me, that I would become the world's finest soldier and would gain a sense of pride and fitness. I didn't know what was going on here at all. I realized that I could never understand this process in all the confusion so I decided to trust my instincts to bring me through. The strongest instinct I had right now was to make myself as anonymous as possible, do all I could to avoid coming face to face with any of the people in charge, and pay strict attention to my surroundings so that I could learn the right and wrong ways to go about staying alive.

The weight of the sack was beginning to take it's toll on my right arm. I itched insanely from the sweat trickling down my back that moved the loose hairs ever so slightly and caused the nerve endings to scream for relief. The terror I had felt gave way to resentment. "Who in the hell do these dirty sonsofbitches think they are? It is completely insane to stand here and take this kind of shit from anybody—I don't care if they are big-ass marines. I sure as hell didn't sign up for this bullshit," I thought to myself. I could feel a rising desire to give verbal expression to my thoughts and knew it was a dangerous course of action, so instead I just seethed inside.

My whole right side hurt from holding the sack. I hated the stupid fartsack. I hated the dirty bastard in back of me for pressing on me. "Probably enjoys it the queer fucker," I thought. I hated the man in front of me for having scales on his lousy skull. I hated the ruthless, lying smoothtalking recruiter who snared me into the whole thing. I silently loathed the disgusting people who ran this joint and were swiftly and certainly taking me apart. My feelings of hate grew more and more intense with every passing moment. I'd never felt like that in my entire life. I was surprised at the magnitude of my hatred. Wave after wave of male-volent emotion rose within me. I began to enjoy it. I silently beamed and radiated from the core of my soul. I felt like an evil radio antenna sending black death signals at my captors. I imagined cutting their hands off and pouring lye on the stumps.

7

Plucking their eyes out with a soup spoon. Shooting, slashing, tearing; their blood and torn flesh, food for vultures circling above. My mind almost snapped, I was saved from the madhouse by a sharp slap on the back of the head.

"Stand up straight, shitbird!" a drill instructor said. I woke up from my reverie and felt strangely refreshed.

I realized now what the full implications of this drama were. It was going to be a sustained and terrible battle—a classic confrontation that every person faces at some point. It was going to be a battle of wits, a mental struggle. To the victor would go the spoils and the spoils of this war was my soul. Losing meant that I would be like one of the madmen running the place. If I won it meant the keeping of my individuality and freedom to think for myself. The battle lines were drawn and the war had begun.

"Awright, ladies, look alive there!" a short, ugly drill sergeant shouted. "Let me introduce myself to you fine young gentlemen," he said, his rough voice dripping with sarcasm. My name is Sgt. Miller and I'm your drill instructor. I own you. You are my little toys to play with for the next few weeks. You will obey me. If you do not obey me and do exactly as you are told while you are here I am empowered to lock you up in the brig. The brig is a very unhappy place to be, girls, and it would behoove you to avoid it. I have locked up many turds before you and I will lock up many turds after you. I LIKE to lock up turds that disobey orders. I also like to thump on turds so plan on getting thumped. When I give you the word you will move into the room directly to your left and take your position in front of a numbered box. Move!"

We scrambled in through the doorway and each found a box, painted green, with a yellow number marked on it.

"I want you to strip off those funny looking clothes you're wearing, maggots. I want every last stitch of civilian clothes off you motherfuckers, pronto! Put the clothes in the box in front of you. Include everything—that means everything. Don't ask to keep your cunt's picture either cause she's already sucking on your best friend's steamer anyhow. Let's go! It's two o'clock in the morning already!"

8

We started ripping our clothes off as quickly as possible while Sgt. Miller and another Sgt. raced up and down the line, screaming, poking, and kicking anyone who tarried. We finally stood at attention, buck naked, the last vestige of pride and civilian identity crumpled and destroyed.

We were moved like cattle to the showers, tired, beaten, and completely dismantled. We sloshed through the ankle deep water that was thick with soap and scum and scrubbed our bodies. We were supervised by a huge black Sgt.

"Scrub the head!" Five seconds.

"Scrub the armpits!" Five seconds.

"Wash the ass down, girls!" "Skin'er back and wash the dickhead, sweethearts!" "OK ladies, rinse!" "Move out! Make way for the next bunch. Move it!"

Out of the showers and back to the box with the number. The shower was wonderful even if it was the fastest one I ever took.

We stood at attention in front of our boxes and waited for the rest of the privates to return from the shower room. Naked and shivering I prayed for invisibility or at least that I would be spared physical injury.

Corporal James, the one who had greeted us outside on the yellow footprints, swaggered into the room and climbed atop a desk at the front.

"Now I'm gonna dress you cocksuckers so listen up real close and you might get some sleep tonight. The first thing I want you pigs to do is reach way down in the fartsack and pull out a pair of skivvy drawers. You probably been calling the goddam things underpanties or some such civilian horseshit but from this day forward you will call them skivvy drawers. Is that understood?"

"Yes, sir!"

"I can't hear you!"

"Yes, sir!" we shouted.

"Good." "Now get them skivvies out and put 'em on."

Piece by piece the Corporal dressed us. When he was finished we were wearing, for the first time, the green fatigues of the U.S. Marines. My beige cloth belt made nearly 1 3/4's revolutions around my waist, the trousers hung over my stiff black boots, and my dick poked through the front opening of my gargantuan skivvy drawers. Most of the other recruits were similarly decked out and, no doubt, looked as ludicrous as I did.

"Looking good assholes. Looking very squared away," Corporal James laughed. "You will now lick the tape provided for the boxes which contain your civilian gear and stick it on over the flaps in a lengthwise direction. The boxes will then be marked with the felt tip pen. Print the address where you wish the box to be sent. Do that now."

I taped my box shut and wrote the address of my parents on it. The sensation of finality was very strong.

"OK people, move out the hatch on the left and proceed to the street. Your drill instructor will take over from there. As of this moment you are no longer who you were when you entered this place. If you don't believe that look in a mirror. Your civilian ways and attitudes no longer exist. They have been taken from you. What you were up to this point is now gone forever. You are nothing! You are zero! You are trash and scum and will continue to be scum until we make you into marines. We have made you nothing and you will thank us when the day comes that you can call yourself a marine! Now get your scuzzy, pukey asses out of my sight!"

We "fell in" on the street where the Corporal had directed us to go. Thirty nothings holding onto our fartsacks and our sanity with the tiny amount of strength that we had left.

Sgt. Miller started marching us to the barracks where we were to live for the remainder of our training. In a matter of seconds our platoon was stumbling along out of step, trying to look military but simply too beaten and overwhelmed and tired to make it. The drill instructor screamed and kicked at the stragglers and eventually we reached our destination.

The Sgt. piled us into the quonset huts, and without blankets, pillows, or sheets had us climb onto the beds. We were still fully dressed.

"It's 0300 hours pukes. I want you dolls to get your beauty rest so when I turn out the lights I want every swinging dick to go to sleep. If I hear any noise you'll be up the rest of the night doing push-ups. Is that clear?"

"Yes sir," we answered.

"I will explain the rules and regulations and what is expected of you tomorrow morning. By the way, tomorrow morning starts in an hour and a half." Snap. Darkness.

In the blackness of the night I tried to collect my thoughts and develop a strategy for coping with the monstrous situation I had gotten myself into. In five seconds I was asleep.

CHAPTER TWO

...And so it was indeed; she was now only ten inches high, and her face brightened up at the thought that she was now the right size for going through the little door into that garden. First, however, she waited for a few minutes to see if she was going to shrink any further: she felt a little nervous about this; "for it might end, you know," said Alice to herself, "in my going out altogether, like a candle....

The morning started out with a bang. A drill sergeant woke us by smashing a fifty gallon garbage can with a length of pipe. The lights were snapped on at the same time and the sergeant was urging us to rise from our short sleep.

"Get up!" Move it, move it, move it, people! Let go a'your cocks and grab your socks. Get the fuck up off your asses, get squared away, and fall in on platoon street!" You have exactly one minute!"

I flew from the bed and did what I could to straighten my clothes up. I was so exhausted that I would have killed for another hour's rest.

I ran out the door and lined up with the others on the ten-foot-wide strip of asphalt that the sergeant had dubbed platoon street. I stood at attention in the darkness of early morning, eyes straight ahead, feet at a forty-five degree angle, thumbs along the seams of the trousers, and an ugly buzz dancing through my body. I didn't know if I was too tired to feel fear or too afraid to feel tired. Either way it was rock bottom as far as I was concerned.

"Good morning, girls."

"Good morning, sir."

"Louder, girls."

"GOOD MORNING, SIR!"

"That's better. The first thing we do around here in the morning is shave. The second thing is exercise. The third thing we do is go to chow."

"GODDAM, BOY," how many times you gotta be told not to move when you're at attention? Get down on your face and give me ten push-ups," he shouted at one of the privates. "When I give you the word you will return to the rack where you slept last night. You will open your mattress cover and you will extract from the mattress cover one razor, one bar of soap, one soap dish with lid, one toothbrush with tooth polish and plastic case. You will also take one towel and one washcloth. When you have gathered these things you will return to platoon street. You have exactly sixty seconds to accomplish this. Do it now."

We ran to our racks and began looking for the named items. In the confusion of the previous night all of my new clothes and gear had gotten mixed up in the bag and I found myself sorting through all of the stuff in the bag to find the shaving equipment. I got everything but the razor. "Where is the damned thing" I thought, mildly irritated. The other turds were starting to file back out to the street and I still couldn't find it. "Maybe I didn't get one," I said to myself.

"You have thirty seconds ladies," the DI growled. Half the platoon was on the street now. I searched the bag frantically and still couldn't find it. "Son of a bitch, of all the luck," I muttered quietly. "Sonofabitch, sonofabitch, sonofabitch."

"Fifteen seconds, sweetpeas!" I could feel my throat constrict with panic. Getting singled out like this the first day was a very bad thing. There! I spotted the silver razor, snatched it from the bag, gathered the rest of the gear and tore out the door. I made it just as the Sergeant walked out of his office.

We marched the half block to the head and were halted outside the door.

"Awright screws, listen carefully. You have ten minutes to get

14

cleaned up. You have permission to piss or shit. When you are finished shitting and pissing you will move into the shower room. You will form lines in front of each sink. You will quickly shave and brush your fangs. It would behoove you to think about the turd waiting for you to finish because if everyone isn't back here in formation on time you will all receive my undivided attention. You have ten minutes from right now. Dismissed."

We dashed into the head and quickly relieved our bladders. No one attempted a bowel movement. Lines formed in front of the washbowls. Razors zipped over cheeks and throats with unchecked speed. Blood flowed everywhere. Arguments developed. At most sinks two recruits at a time dipped their razors and jockeyed for position. It was a madhouse.

Sergeant Miller waited patiently as the ten-minute limit came and went. It was nearly fifteen minutes before the last man came running from the head.

We marched back to the quonset huts and stowed our shaving gear. The drill instructor calmly waited as we lined up again.

"You girls have disobeyed a direct order from a noncommissioned officer," he began quietly. "Perhaps because you have just arrived here you are unaware of the seriousness of your crime. I am, quite frankly, disappointed. I feel that it would be a waste of the Corps' resources to lock all of you up so I must make my point in another manner."

I thought to myself that Sergeant Miller had made a complete switch of personality. There was something ominous about such a drastic change from cursing and extreme aggressiveness to cool sophistication.

"Please spread out and get down in the push-up position," he said. We squirmed around until everyone was down. The DI then began counting for us.

"Down-one. Down-two. Down-three...." The limit for most of us was about ten push-ups. One private started to sag about the fifth repetition.

"You weak, piss-ant cunt you!" Straighten that yellow backbone out or so help me god I'll break you right in half!"

"Down-four." Sergeant Miller worked us over. When we could

15

no longer even attempt to do push-ups he had us do squat bends. When that became impossible he had us roll over and over until we were scratched and bleeding and dirty. In less than a half hour he reduced us to quivering, slobbering, prideless pieces of meat. Many privates were actually sobbing with pain and fear and frustration. Several even cried out "Please!" or "Stop!"

"Tensh-hut!" We crawled to our feet and got at attention.

"The next time I give you girls an order, are you going to obey that order or disobey that order?" Sergeant Miller asked.

"Obey, sir!"

"What?"

"Obey, sir!"

"I can't hear you, maggots!"

"OBEY, SIR!!" our voices rang as one all the way across the huge drill field and echoed back.

"Good. We will get along much better if you do."

We marched off to chow, chastened and determined not to disobey Sergeant Miller again.

At the mess hall we sidestepped through the line, then moved to the long tables designated by the DI. We were directed to put our tin trays on the table and stand at attention. When the entire platoon was thus assembled the DI bellowed, "Ready...seats." We practiced that fifteen or twenty times until he was satisfied with our precision and then we ate the cold, evil mush in record time.

The food consisted of diced potatoes, bits of rutabaga, pieces of hamburger, and ketchup. I gagged but managed to clean my plate as ordered.

When we walked out of the mess hall the sky was streaked red and gold by the rising sun.

Sergeant Miller herded us to the platoon area and we joined up on platoon street with another group of about thirty privates. Apparently that group had arrived at a different time and were processed into the recruit depot after us. Instead of thirty nothings we were now sixty nothings. This was fine with me as it made it twice as easy to avoid being singled out or noticed as an individual.

We cleaned the quonset huts and head and were assigned bunks and footlockers. This took about an hour and was confusing but quiet. After that we were ordered out on the street.

A sergeant stepped out of the DI hut and walked up and down the narrow street between the two lines that we had formed. He was older than Sergeant Miller but in just as good condition physically. He had the same type of haircut as the other DIs we had seen, bald on the sides. The top of his head was covered with a smoky bear hat, which was cocked forward and held in place by a thin black leather strap around the back of his skull. He was about six feet tall and had the tanned, deeply creased appearance that is unique to Marine drill instructors.

The most striking feature of this new sergeant were his eyes. They were dark brown and abnormally wide open. He looked as though he had been startled at some time and remained puzzled ever since. I didn't realize then that I would see the same type of eyes again very soon. At least half of the marines in Vietnam had the same look after their first taste of death in the jungle, but only a very small percentage of men were left with that expression permanently impressed on their features. The "look" seemed to indicate that the person had not yet made up his mind whether he was the stalker or the stalked.

The new DI introduced himself as Sergeant Barton and gave us a brief lecture on what he expected of us. He seemed controlled and almost mild as he explained that he was the senior DI and would be known as the Platoon Commander. It was obvious that this man was not a screamer like all the other marines we had encountered thus far and apparently several privates found this fact too tempting to pass over. There was movement in the ranks.

"OK, well, fine then, if that's the way you want to have it it's fine with me," said Sergeant Barton calmly. "Get down on your fucking faces."

We got in the push-up position. The DI counted out ten push-ups and then had us hold the "up" position. Arms trembled, shook and collapsed. Recruits grunted and moaned.

"So then, that's it I guess. You girls like to mill around instead of standing at attention when I talk to you. You would rather

17

stand on one foot like a cunt than stand at attention like a marine. I suppose you'll just have to learn the hard way," he said. "One-down, two-down"...twenty more minutes of groveling in the dirt taught us that Sergeant Barton was not a pushover. "On your feet," he barked.

We were aware that this man did not wish to strain himself by making a lot of loud noise. He would rather accomplish the objective by straining us.

We got back to attention and this time did not move. He repeated some of the rules of recruit training that we had already learned and explained others that we hadn't gotten as of yet. The first word out of a turd's mouth was "sir." There was no such thing as going to the bathroom or anywhere else alone. Everyone would shit and piss at the same time except in grave emergency. No smoking unless the "smoking lamp" was lit and the only one who could light the lamp was an instructor. When passing anyone except another turd permission would be requested by saying, "Sir by your leave." Shave in the morning, shower at night. No walking except in formation. You run everywhere. No talking at any time to another turd except during the fifteen minutes free time before lights out. If a turd wanted to speak to an instructor he must first request permission.

"In other words," he said, "You don't walk, talk, chew gum, eat, look around, change your clothes, wash, shave, shit, piss, or think unless you are told to do so and supervised while you are doing it. If there's anything I've missed don't do that either."

A marine came out of the DI hut. He was about six-feet-three-inches tall and could best be described as lean. From smokey bear cover to sparkling spitshined shoes he was razor perfect. I instinctively knew that he was the meanest, toughest, most overwhelming man I had ever seen. He stood in front of the group with his massive fists on his hips, his lantern jaw jutting belligerently forward, and a menacing smile on his thin lips. The silence deepened.

I could feel the slight amount of confidence that had been built up by the relatively easygoing Sergeant Barton evaporate. By this time I half believed that I actually was a turd and for sure knew

18

that I wasn't the person who had come in here a short while previously. I had no idea what or who I would be in the future. On the other hand, this man knew exactly where he stood with the world and, more important, what his relationship was to this group of turds in front of him. From the shaky mental ground I was standing on the new DI looked omnipotent.

Sergeant Barton introduced the man as Sergeant Liebermann, and quietly walked back into his office. Sergeant Liebermann took a step forward and dropped his arms to his sides. His hands formed loose fists and he bounced lightly, like a boxer.

When he addressed us his voice was a rasping snarl. "Let me have one turd with a black belt." He was referring to the highest level of karate or judo. No one moved. "No karate experts here? OK, give me one boxer." Silence. "I want a ghetto hard ass to step up here and get his fucking teeth kicked out." Still no movement in the ranks.

"Let's get something straight right now," he spit out. Every one of you is a slimy fuckin' turd. You are totally worthless to me and to the Marine Corps and you will be regarded as such until you become of some value. I'm gonna kick your ass up to your ears every chance I get and I'm gonna get to everyone sooner or later! The first one to fuck up today and the last one to fuck up eleven weeks from now is gonna get my fist right in his fucking face. There are only three ways that you're gonna leave this place. One is to get sent to jail for fucking up. The other is to leave in a pine box. The last and easiest way is to leave here as a marine. My job is to make you pukes sweat blood and I'm gonna fuckin' a do it!" He paused to survey us. He gritted his teeth and said quietly, "Don't cross me!"

The intent of Sergeant Leonard Liebermann was abundantly clear.

The platoon commander came back out and, working with DI Liebermann, got us arranged in an orderly fashion, tallest recruits in the front, shortest in the rear. I fitted in about the middle and was grateful for my average height.

We marched to the other side of the drill field, stopping three times to do push-ups when the DIs got exasperated with our lack of coordination. Sergeant Barton called cadence while Sergeant Liebermann roamed about slashing recruits with both his hands and his words.

"Get in step!"

"Align yourself to the right!"

"Wake up you dumb spaghetti-eatin mother-fuckin' wop!"

Eventually we made it to the other side and it seemed like a major accomplishment. We lined up outside a large quonset hut that was being used as a photographic studio and had the appearance of an airplane hangar. We were taken inside one by one to get photos taken for our ID cards. It was a slow process and I could feel the fatigue seeping into my brain.

I started to drift off and pulled myself together. Against my will the dreams crowded in. I lost track of the present and was asleep standing up. I dreamed that the DIs had a make-up room in the wings and all that had happened was merely a play with very accomplished actors.

"Get over here, asshole!" I woke up and slowly sneaked my way back to attention.

"That's right boy, I'm talking to you."

I knew deep down that he wanted me but I didn't dare look over at him.

"You don't get over here in five seconds son I'm gonna send you to the jailhouse."

I had to look. A quick peek confirmed my fears. Sergeant Liebermann was looking right at me. So I was going to be the first one to get blasted. A surge of anger went through me. "I've had it with this shit. I'll show this nut that he doesn't scare me a bit," I thought. I broke from the rank and trotted over to the DI.

"Sir, Private O'Brian reporting as ordered." I looked him straight in the eye defiantly. I expected that the look I gave him would cause Sergeant Liebermann to back off and leave me alone.

The DI narrowed his eyes and hissed, "Take your fuckin' eyeballs off me, puke!" For some unknown reason the DI's use of the word "eyeballs" threw me off. I could have withstood the word eyes and maintained my defiant posture but the very graphicness of "eyeballs" drained me of the fragile energy I had summoned for the confrontation and left me at the drill instructor's disposal.

"Report to me when we get back to the area. Now git!" he spat out. I spun on my heel and ran back to the formation.

I had a sick feeling in my stomach and a greater understanding of just how powerless we really were.

It was only mid-morning of the first training day and my attempt at rebellion had been squashed with ridiculous ease. So far, in less than twenty-four hours, our normal state of mind had been completely altered. Our sense of time was shattered. An hour was like a day or a hundred years. The spaces we could enter or leave were determined entirely by our DIs. Our normal sense of self was destroyed. Our minds were occupied with the noise and disorder of the drill instructor's screams so there was no room in our heads for ideas that were not put there by the deliberate design of our instructors. I didn't see this relationship of the platoon to the instructors as one of trainees to trainers and I'm certain that most of the platoon didn't either. When stripped of its trappings it became very evident that our relationship was, and would continue to be, that of the keeper and the kept.

❦   ❦   ❦

August, 1965   Chu Lai, South Vietnam
(Staff Sergeant Cavanaugh has us in the hold of the LST, one of those hulking navy ships that are designed to carry men and equipment to landing areas for amphibious assaults. Cavanaugh is a beady-eyed man who loves his job and himself and hates everything else. I don't care much for him but I trust his judgment because he's been through all this before and seems to know as much about it as anyone.)

He told us the basic plan for the landing that would take place the next morning and said that the plan would get all fucked up as soon as the shit hit the fan, so we shouldn't panic. "Just stick with your unit," he said, "and make your shots count." He started to go into a pep talk about how it was the moment of truth

21

for us but stopped when he saw that nobody was interested. He dismissed us.

Up on deck we could hear the booming of artillery and navy guns. It reminded me of August in Minnesota. First a sharp flash of lightning, then a thunderclap. The only difference was that the air would rush over us shortly after the huge shells exploded, giving us a small taste of the concussion that was absorbed by our enemy.

After a while I went down into the sleeping quarters to rest. I thought about the guy in *The Red Badge of Courage* and how, before his first battle, he worried about the way he would behave when confronted with death. It seemed to me that the soldier had the whole thing overrated. I felt no fear of death. I was not worried about running away from the enemy or not being able to perform. The one thing I felt afraid of was hurting my spine.

It was still dark when they woke us up for breakfast. We hustled through the meal and went topside for our gear. After hurrying for fifteen minutes we sat down on the packs and waited for an hour while the sailors got the small boats ready for us. During the wait we talked and cleaned imaginary dirt from our weapons. Some played cards or wrote letters.

Finally, the company gunnery sergeant gave us the word to saddle up. I strapped on my .45 caliber pistol, slipped the pack and radio on my back, picked up the clumsy M-14 rifle, and went over the side of the LST. We climbed down the rope ladder three men at a time and eventually the small boat was filled and we were churning through the choppy waters of the South China Sea.

Having my mind filled to overflow with visions of the landings at Tarawa and Iwo Jima, I expected a full-blown battle at the beach. The flap in front of the landing craft dropped as soon as we hit sand and we scrambled out, peeling off to the left and right with rifles at the ready. Instead of being met with a barrage of mortars and small arms fire we were greeted by the curious stares of a dozen old women dressed in black pajamas, straw hats, and bare feet. We ignored them and walked to our predesignated position about five hundred yards inland from the beach. We settled down in a clump of lacy pine trees—which was the only vegetation that the sandy soil would permit—and waited some more.

I remember laughing with Whitmore and Lucas about the sand we were sitting in. We'd had days and days of lectures and practice on jungle warfare; everything we had been taught was about the jungle, and here we were, in Vietnam, up to our ass in powdery sand. There was a small runway several hundred yards to our north that was made of giant metal planks linked together. Sand everywhere. For the first time I had a stab of apprehension in my belly. They hadn't said a goddam word about sand and I didn't know how to kill or be killed in sand.

Finally we got the order to move out. I stuck to the platoon commander, Lieutenant Phillips, like glue. We walked for perhaps five miles while the sun got hotter and the sand slowly gave way to thick vegetation.

"Panzer Charlie 2 Actual, this is Panzer Actual, over." I reached up and took the headset off the hook on my right shoulder and handed it to the Lieutenant. It was the Company Commander. He asked for our location. The Lieutenant gave our coordinates from his map and was told to take us to another position about a mile south and hook up with our company. We started for the area mentioned and after about ten minutes we heard gunfire. The Lieutenant put us in double time and we ran along a path until we made contact with Charlie company on the radio. Lieutenant Phillips and Captain Rahm, the Company Commander, discussed the situation and what they agreed upon caused a strange thrill in my throat.

The first and third platoons had made contact with an estimated twenty-five VC. The guerrillas had just broken off and the main body was coming toward our position. There were an estimated fifteen men and we were to set up an ambush.

We took the positions that we had practiced so many times. First and second squads on the right, third squad forming the base of the "L." A fire team went fifty yards up the trail as a listening post. Machine guns were placed straight ahead so the

VC couldn't run. Corporal Mackey was at the exact point of fire concentration with a sawed-off, double-barreled twelve-gauge shotgun to level the first blast.

We could not have been any quieter. Not a sound, not a squeak or a rustle came from any man in the platoon. I turned the radio off and waited. My heart was pounding. The main thing I felt was an overwhelming sense of having the upper hand. The gooks were walking into a trap like lambs to the slaughterhouse and we all knew it.

The other thing I felt, and I am going to admit it despite my deep reluctance to do so, was a sexual sensation. As an aside, I was fortunate to have known other men well enough to have learned that my sexual reaction to the stimulus of killing (or more politely, "combat") was not just a personal aberration but was in fact quite common.

The few minutes of waiting for the gooks to arrive were filled with an insane sense of power. I had learned from a very early age that the ultimate loss was the loss of one's life. Therefore the ultimate win was to take another's life by force. A whole generation, mine, had been fed a steady diet, via the TV and school programming, of John Wayne, the Lone Ranger, the FBI, George Washington, General Patton, and other violent symbols of manhood. We learned, in no uncertain terms, that a real man slashed, chops and shoots the life out of his enemy and is nice to women, children and pets of the canine variety. The training in the Marines was an intensification of that line of reasoning and, like it or not, the ideas and symbols that had been ingrained in our very souls were about to explode forth in the form of bullets, grenades, and buckshot.

The leader of the listening post fire team gave the hand signal for "contact imminent" and even the breathing seemed to be suspended. Seconds later, a Viet Cong came down the middle of the path. I could see him clearly. He was in a hurry. His youth surprised me. Barely fourteen or so. Carrying an old bolt action rifle. Black pajamas, bare head, shiny, uncut hair. Experienced eyes flashing. We let him pass.

24

The rest followed, maybe twenty yards behind the point man. There were thirteen of them. They were in single file and every man was holding his out-of-date rifle in a direction opposite the man in front, thereby covering both sides of the path. They didn't seem dangerous at all. In fact, they looked comical with their baggy black clothes and old guns.

The leader of the column reached Mackey's position. The air shattered and the blast from both barrels shredded the little guy from his waist up. The flesh and blood and bits of bone exploded from his body and left a ravaged dead man standing there. For perhaps half a second the body of the man made an attempt to get away, or perhaps it was trying to recover its torn flesh. Then it crumpled and lay still.

Within a second or two of Mackey's shot the entire platoon opened fire. The withering sheet of burning steel lasted less than ten seconds. Lieutenant Phillips gave a cease fire and we came out of our spots. Thirteen men lay dead, their blood spilling out so fast that it didn't even run, but instead formed thick pools.

We waited for Smith's fire team to return with the point man. In a minute or two they came down the path dragging the boy by his heels. They added him to the pile. The smell of the blood and gunpowder was overwhelming.

Lieutenant Phillips gave us a grin and said, "Let's saddle up and get the fuck out of here." We grabbed our gear and headed toward Charlie company with the blood from our first encounter still wet on the ground. The trembling that I felt was the result of a massive dose of adrenalin.

❧   ❧   ❧

When the photo session was finished we returned to the platoon area and received explicit instructions on how to make our beds, clean the barracks, manicure the grounds and so on. Each activity seemed to involve intricate, detailed perfection.

I decided not to report to the DI as ordered. For some reason I had the feeling that he would forget that he had told me to see him when we returned so, relying on my intuition, I lay back and hoped.

"Private O'Brian to the duty hut!" came the shout from the DI office.

"Sir, Private O'Brian to the duty hut, aye, aye, sir," the platoon echoed. We had been told to repeat any order coming from the duty hut.

I ran to the hut, thinking up excuses along the way. On the wall next to the door was a wooden slab with directions written on it concerning the proper protocol to use when reporting to a DI.

Following the directions I pounded three times. "Sir, Private O'Brian requests permission to enter the duty hut."

"Try it again, boy."

Three more knocks. "Sir, Private O'Brian requests permission to enter the duty hut."

"Try it again, boy."

I went through the procedure about six times before the DI said to come in.

"Sir, Private O'Brian requests permission to speak."

"Speak."

Standing in front of his desk I kept my eyes on the sign that read, "Woe unto those who enter here." "Sir, Private O'Brian reporting as ordered."

"Who ordered you turd?"

"Sir, you did."

"Ewe! Do I look like a ewe? Do I look like a goddam sheep, private?"

I was puzzled. "No, sir."

"A ewe is a female sheep, Private O'Brian. Do I look like a female sheep?"

"No, sir."

"Who ordered you to report, fuckstick?"

"Sir, the drill instructor did, sir." My eyes shifted for a fraction of a second.

"What are you looking at, private?"

"Sir, I wasn't looking at anything, sir."

"You like to look around don't you?"

"No, sir."

26

"Why didn't you report to me when we got back, scum?"

"Sir, I was waiting for a break."

"There's no such thing as a break here. The only thing that's gonna break is your face when I kick it in!"

"Yes, sir."

"Why were you looking at me during the photo session?"

"Sir, I don't know." I didn't dare contradict him.

"You queer for me, boy?"

"No, sir."

"You call me a sheep and look me over. You ever fuck a sheep, O'Brian?"

"No, sir."

Sergeant Miller and Sergeant Barton had quietly drifted into the room and I could see them smiling out of the corner of my eye.

"Do you like me, Private O'Brian?"

I was stuck. "Yes, sir."

The other two DIs moved in on me.

"You a faggot ain't you laddy?" Sergeant Miller asked, his face six inches from my ear.

"No, sir."

"You wanna get a fat, hard cock up your shit tube, you pukey fuckin' queer?" yelled Sergeant Barton.

"No, sir."

"You just said you liked me. Have you been telling me lies, boy?"

"No, sir."

"You do like me then huh, queer?"

"No, sir."

"You got a funny feeling for my ass?"

"You want me to fuck you?"

"Tell the truth faggot or we'll lock you up tight!"

"Faggot?" Motherfucking faggot!"

"Sheepfuckin' queer cocksucker!"

The three DIs had surrounded me and were screaming in my face, threatening me with prison and a dishonorable discharge and my name in every police station in the United States because I was a sex pervert.

27

"You wanna eyeball me some more, private?"

"No, sir."

Sergeant Liebermann hit me in the chest with a short jolting right hand punch. The others kicked and punched me in the back and in the legs until I went down.

"Get up on your feet, asshole." I did.

Sergeant Liebermann looked at the platoon commander. "Should I call the MPs and have him locked up?"

I was actually worried that somehow I would be spirited away and locked up in the brig.

"Let's just keep an eye on him for now," Sergeant Barton replied.

The DI nodded. "Would you like your parents notified that we've discovered you're a homosexual, Private O'Brian?"

I almost burst into tears. "Sir, I'm not!" I cried out.

"Then you keep your fuckin' eyes off me when you're at a position of attention, understand?" he yelled.

"Yes, sir."

"I'm making you my house mouse, shitbird, you got that?"

"Aye, aye, sir."

"Get the fuck out of my sight!"

"Aye, aye, sir." I did an about face and ran back outside with a firm resolve to avoid notice at all costs in the future.

Platoon 211 was across the street in the sand pit. They were crawling, hands behind their backs, looking for a skyhook that one of the drill instructors had lost. I joined in the search, happy to be part of the group. Being an individual, I had learned, was a very dangerous way to live.

CHAPTER THREE

"Come, there's no use in crying like that!" said Alice to herself, rather sharply; "I advise you to leave off this minute!" She generally gave herself very good advice (though she very seldom followed it), and sometimes she scolded herself so severely as to bring tears into her eyes; and once she remembered trying to box her own ears for having cheated herself in a game of croquet she was playing against herself, for this curious child was very fond of pretending to be two people. "But it's no use now," thought poor Alice, "to pretend to be two people! Why, there's hardly enough of me left to make one respectable person!"

The first three days of boot camp passed with agonizing slowness. Routine procedures such as dental checkup, shots, psychiatric exams, and aptitude tests were used as a vehicle for teaching us that any violation of discipline was immediate cause for punishment.

Each time a mistake occurred we did physical exercises until the majority of recruits could not perform any more. Our bodies ached from head to toe and without even being aware of it we were being whipped into a state of health and fitness.

The main point that was stressed the first few days was breaking down any resistance that may have cropped up as concerned the keeping of individuality. This was done in part by removing the natural social barriers that we had. What a "civilian" considered privacy was outlawed completely in training. There was great emphasis on doing everything as a group and nothing as a lone person.

For the first week I didn't even attempt to empty my bowels. Very few privates did. Then, when it started to hurt, I couldn't go. In the first place we never got enough time to do the job properly since we had brought to boot camp the casual elimination habits of civilian life. Second, most of us had a natural sensitivity about squatting on a toilet in the middle of a crowd. However, in a few days, during the half hour that we had for hygiene at night, all twenty-four toilets were covered by the eager asses of Platoon 211. I was amazed at how unconcerned I had become about sitting on a seatless toilet with eleven people next to me and a dozen directly facing me, all of us staring into space and grunting and shitting to our hearts' content. I even grew accustomed to using the third stool on the right side and came to regard it as my own.

Another private thing that was strictly forbidden was masturbating. Sgt. Miller explained to us that if he heard any racks squeaking in the night he would find out who was beating his hammer and have him arrested on the spot. Since the General had not entered a time slot in the schedule for jacking off we would not be doing that, and anyway if one turd jacked off everybody should jack off and our mothers wouldn't like that idea. So that was that.

When the physicals and so forth were finished we started in on our regular training program. This consisted of marching and classes. More marching and classes. And marching. We spent hour after hour on the drill field, or grinder, going over the close order drill maneuvers. The drill instructors alternately raved and explained patiently. By the end of the first week we could march in step and do all of the drills fairly efficiently. Oddly enough, when I had signed up for the Marines I had no idea that there would be marching involved in recruit training. I was disappointed and disillusioned to find that marching was almost the only thing that we did. I was beginning to see that the Marine Corps was not for me.

I had made enough progress as a house mouse during the

opening week so that I was relieved by Private Weslin, a red-haired recruit from Iowa. My duties as a house mouse were to clean the DIs' hut and attend to their personal gear while the rest of 211 was cleaning up the platoon area. During this time I had the opportunity to observe and absorb all the information that I could.

The privacy of the recruits wasn't the only privacy that was being violated, I learned. The DIs had to live in a manner that the average person would never tolerate. Although they had far more freedom and personal choice than recruits about the basic things in life they still had to wear the uniforms they were told to wear, cut their hair as they were told, come in for duty at odd hours, and other things that most people would consider abnormal infringements on personal life.

I also learned a very important thing because of my house mouse status. I saw the DIs with their guard down. I saw and heard them talking and joking about baseball, women, fishing, their families, and other everyday concerns of the real world. I noted their dirty linen and rumpled socks and letters starting with their first names. It was very, very significant to me that the DIs, regardless of the illusion to the contrary, were real people with real lives. Only a house mouse would know that because every time the rest of the platoon saw a DI he was dressed, made up, and played his well-rehearsed role perfectly.

After I was relieved as a house mouse I never got another glimpse of the DIs human stature but, fortunately, that information was already in my mental file.

On Sunday we followed the normal routine: reveille at 0430 hours, calisthenics, two-mile run, morning hygiene and off to breakfast. We came back from breakfast and instead of getting our rifles and doing close order drill, as we had usually done, we were told to change into clean uniforms and report back on the street in five minutes.

Sgt. Liebermann, who was on duty that day, stood in front of Platoon 211. "Awright fuckers, seeing as we want to stay as close to your recruiter's promises as possible"...a muffled laugh from the platoon..."We are going to keep one of his promises today.

31

The Marine Corps builds men in body, mind, and spirit, as I'm sure your recruiter told you. Well, today and every Sunday from now on we are going to work on your spirits. You will believe in God each and every Sunday of your training. I don't give a fuck if you never believed before, you will believe now. I don't give a shit if you never even thought of praising the Lord—you will praise anyhow. There are two services, Catholic and Protestant. You will pick one and attend. You may not attend both. You will pray! You will listen to the chaplain! And may the Almighty Lord save your fucking souls!" He paused, obviously pleased with himself. "The smoking lamp is lit for one cigarette!"

"Sir," we sang, "The smoking lamp is lit for one cigarette. Aye, aye, sir."

"Get 'em and light 'em up."

"Sir, get 'em and light 'em up. Aye, aye, sir." We scrambled for cigarettes. This was too much to even have hoped for.

Our morale was sky high as we dragged deeply on our cigarettes, making ourselves dizzy after so long an absence. Bliss!

"Put 'em out," said the DI after several minutes.

"Sir, put 'em out. Aye, aye, sir." We cheerfully dropped the butts in the bucket that a recruit was carrying up and down the ranks.

"All mackerel snatchers fall in on the grinder. That's Catholics to you dumb ones."

I fell in with the Catholics and Sgt. Liebermann marched us over to the base theatre where Sunday services were held. We filed in and took our seats. The deep, plush seat was the first comfortable chair I had felt since the plane ride to San Diego. The lights dimmed and the soothing, Latin monotone echoed softly through the theatre as the chaplain, dressed in his colorful robes, began the mass. I was thankful for the quiet and the dark.

I thought back to when I was a young boy and walked two miles to church every day. Each day I would pray and each day my tender boyhood emotions would be healed and uplifted by the calm atmosphere, rich wood and marble, beautiful ceremony, and most of all by the thought that there was a Perfect Being who poured his love out to me without limit or justification.

I suppressed a rush of tears as that feeling came over me in the theatre. The psychological defenses that I had built up during the previous week came apart in that warm and quiet place. The vicious screaming and chaos had caused a wall of resistance and the more brutal the harassment had been the stronger the resistance had become. When the force and pressure had suddenly ceased and was replaced with its opposite the mental wall came crashing down. It was an awesome process.

After a couple of minutes of trauma I realized what was happening. I was not being held in the hand of the Lord at all. I was merely in the eye of the hurricane.

We put our scrub buckets upside down and sat on them while the Protestants were at church. We shined our boots and belt buckles and cleaned our rifles. This was a welcome change of pace from the normal schedule.

When the Protestants returned from church we put our buckets away and lined up on the street. The DI, whose disposition had darkened considerably, paced slowly up and down.

"Private Johnson, front and center," he called.

"Sir, Private Johnson, front and center."

Johnson, whom I had spotted as a rebel earlier, stepped from the formation and reported to the DI.

"Private Johnson, did you attend Sunday services this morning?"

"No, sir."

"Why not, Private Johnson?"

"I don't believe in God, sir."

"Did I tell you to believe in God, Private Johnson?"

"Yes, sir."

"Did I tell you to attend church this morning, Private Johnson?"

"Yes, sir."

"It makes me very unhappy to see my turds disobeying my lawful direct orders, Private Johnson. Do you realize that?"

"Yes, sir."

"I am not going to physically punish you, Private Johnson, because I don't think you are worth it."

33

"Aye, aye, sir."

"Anything you say may be used against you in a legally declared court martial, you may remain silent, and you may procure the services of a civilian attorney, is that understood?"

"Yes, sir." Spoken defiantly.

The drill instructor nodded toward his office door and two burly marines came out. They were wearing armbands with the letters MP embroidered on them. One drew out a leaded night stick and stood in front of the recruit with feet spread apart while the other MP moved around behind him. The one in back grabbed Johnson's arms, pulled them behind his back, whipped out a pair of silver handcuffs and snapped them on his wrists. Johnson's eyes bulged as he was hustled away by the military police.

Platoon 211 was made uncomfortable by the display of power we had jut seen but we weren't actually surprised. After all, the DIs had been promising to lock someone up for a week and now it had happened. What we didn't know was just how far the MPs would go in their punishment of the luckless private. It was conceivable that his one foolish action of skipping church could result in several years confinement at hard labor, although that seemed unlikely. One thing that we all appeared to be in agreement with was the idea that it was "better him than me."

That night, during our fifteen minute free period, I noticed a disturbing change in the platoon. The DIs were fairly tolerant by that time of quiet conversation during free time and the main topic was Private Johnson.

"Hey, they just hauled him away, just like that," said one of the recruits from California, a pleasant young man named Jim Young.

"Well, that's his own problem, he disobeyed an order. The rest of us had to go so he should've gone too. Fuck 'im," said another recruit.

Private Young answered with, "Yeah, but it's pretty extreme, don't you think?"

"He got what he deserved."

"That's right. Piss on him."

"Johnson wasn't with the program anyway."

A dozen other voices murmured assent.

The training was gaining a foothold in the minds of my fellow turds. It was plain to see that some of the men in 211 either enjoyed the humiliation and brutality or else figured that the best way to survive the ordeal was to submit to the programming and embrace it in the same way that many people accept life styles that are obviously unpleasant or downright painful.

I kept out of the conversation and made a mental note to mask my sentiments while in the company of platoon members, as well as in the presence of the instructors.

The next morning we stopped drilling about nine o'clock and were marched to a set of bleachers that were situated in a remote corner of the base and seemed to have no purpose. The bleachers faced a large pile of rocks and about fifty yards to the right was a smaller pile of rock chips. We were not told the reason for our presence there.

After about a ten-minute wait the sound of a platoon running in step came into the range of our hearing. The rhythmic slap of boots on pavement told us the group was coming at us and was, no doubt, the reason for us being seated in that odd spot.

When they came into sight we could see that each man carried a five-gallon bucket in his left hand and a twenty-pound sledge hammer in his right. They wore blue helmet liners and the normal green utility uniform with the exception of the word BRIG stencilled across the back. The huge black corporal in charge halted the group at the large rock pile. He formed the platoon into teams, one sledge hammer and one bucket man per team.

The big black man turned around and gave us a great, gap-toothed grin. He was wearing a .45 caliber pistol in a shoulder holster and had a loaded submachine gun slung across his chest. He waved cheerfully.

When he gave the order to start each hammer man began slamming the large rock in front of him with tremendous force, splitting the rock and causing dust and chips to fly. The bucket men scrambled to pick up the chips, fill the buckets, and run, grunting and straining, to the smaller pile on the right.

The concussion of the heavy hammers hitting the rocks could be felt all the way to the place where we were sitting.

We watched the operation for about twenty minutes and then went back to drill. Not a word was said by the DIs.

    ❧   ❧   ❧

October, 1965
Chu Lai, South Vietnam

It turned out that the ambush on the first day of the landing was the only visual contact we were to make with "Charlie" for over a month. Charlie had a way of being invisibly present in a most unusual way. He was more a black and terrible ghost than he was human being. Each time one of our men tripped a booby trap it seemed like the haunting spectre of our unseen enemy was laughing in the wind.

The training that was provided us by the Marine Corps had prepared me to accept the inevitable land mines, hidden grenades, and punji stakes. Thus my reaction to the sight of our people being maimed in the "normal" fashion was subdued. There were perhaps a dozen casualties by booby trap the first month, no deaths.

Then, in a matter of a day, the entire concept I had of Victor Charlie changed.

We were on a routine patrol to a small village. The entire purpose of our casual procession was to let the villagers know that we were there and would allow no dealings by them with the VC. We had already covered the same route at least five times and all of us knew what was going to happen—nothing.

James Washington, one of the many blacks in Charlie Company, was the point man. He was about twenty yards ahead of the squad. It was raining and we were covered by our green ponchos, the hoods pulled up around our necks to keep the rain out. The only thing I can think of was that Washington was bundled up in his poncho so snugly that he didn't have enough room to look around carefully. He walked right into a clear fishline that was used as a trip wire. There was a "whoosh" of something rushing through the air and then a loud "thud!" I looked to the front of the column and there was Washington, down on his knees, squealing like a wounded animal and clutching a long branch that bisected the trail. I immediately knew that he was hurt but couldn't understand how it had happened without benefit of the usual explosion.

We ran up to where he was kneeling to help him. By the time we got there Washington was whimpering, begging for help. He was calling for us to take it out.

"Take it out! Please! Please! Get the motherfucker out! please!" The pain was already causing him to stiffen up as people do when badly injured. His skin was turning to an ashen gray right before our eyes.

Doc Turner, our corpsman, slowly straightened the wounded man up. At the end of the branch he was holding onto was a stake approximately two inches in diameter. The VC had tied the huge, sharp stake onto the branch and then stretched it back until there was enough tension to cause the branch to whip out across the trail when the trip wire was released. Washington was unlucky enough to have caught the stake in the middle of the belly.

By the time we got the stake cut loose from the branch Washington was throwing up great heaps of vomit and blood. In less than two minutes from the time he was cut loose he was dead. Apparently the stake had slashed an artery inside his belly.

The doc put one muddy boot on Washington's chest and pulled hard on the stake. It took both hands to remove it. It was stuck at least eight inches deep into the man's guts.

At that moment I realized that we were at war. The cold-blooded rage that must have inspired such a monstrous weapon chilled me to the very marrow of my bones. For the first time I knew that the unfettered violence of the ghosts was intended to be received by me personally. Charlie wanted me dead in the mud, twisted in an agony that can only be imagined. Now the thing started. The fear. I wanted to live. More than a fancy home or a

Cadillac or money. More than love and a wonderful family. I had always had certain qualifications on the way I wanted to live and now those standards were erased as Washington was erased. I didn't give a damn how I lived as long as I was allowed to continue to exist.

The fear was like an extra body part. It was like a cold growth in the pit of the belly that increased and decreased as circumstances changed but never went away entirely. The growth seemed to have a life of its own that said it was better to have Washington die a thousand deaths, a thousand painful, sorrowful, miserable, lonely deaths than to have me die once. The new awareness also said to give Charlie no leeway, no slack whatsoever, when it was him or me that would give up living. Be it man or woman, child or grandpa or brother or sister, the other motherfucker was going to the hole in the ground before me. I wasn't even eighteen years old and I wasn't about to explore the world beyond the grave just yet.

CHAPTER FOUR

It was all very well to say "Drink me," but the wise little Alice was not going to do that in a hurry. "No, I'll look first," she said, "and see whether it's marked 'poison' or not"; for she had read several nice little stories about children who had got burnt, and eaten up by wild beasts and other unpleasant things, all because they would not remember the simple rules their friends had taught them; such as, that a red-hot poker will burn you if you hold it too long; and that if you cut your finger very deeply with a knife, it usually bleeds; and she had never forgotten that, if you drink much from a bottle marked "poison," it is almost certain to disagree with you, sooner or later.

Gary Scriver was next to me in the second squad, and as a result of the whispered remarks that we exchanged when the DI wasn't looking we formed a fast friendship. He was of the same mind regarding our training so it was not dangerous to speak to him.

One thing that bothered Scriver deeply was that he had signed a six-year contract for active duty and now he was stuck with it. Since I had signed for four years it was a minor consolation.

The one quality that Scriver had that stood out was a certain boldness. Like the lifer in prison he must have figured that he had nothing to lose so he managed to assert his independence in various ways, not the least of which was sneaking cigarettes. This was probably the worst crime of all because it was a direct and almost antagonistic violation of the drill instructor's domain.

The DIs were the only ones in the world who had the power to light the smoking lamp and they used it as a reward or punishment. Bypassing the DI and lighting the lamp on one's own was almost unimaginable. By the second week Private Scriver was doing it regularly and seemed impervious to the fact that he was flirting with brig time.

When Scriver invited me to participate in an illicit smoke I could not refuse. Although it was against my better judgment it was almost imperative that I do something to convince myself that I was holding up to the onslaught of the training and that I could make a decision on my own.

That night at shower time I followed Scriver's suggested plan. I tore the filter off of my cigarette, took one match and a small patch of the match striker, put a dab of toothpaste on my finger and headed for the showers with the rest of 211. The DI returned to his hut after dismissing us into the head and instead of going straight in Gary and I lagged behind and at the last minute darted in back of the head. I lit the one match and we got our cigarette going. We gulped it down in about two minutes, scattered the ashes, swallowed the butt and other paraphernalia, licked the toothpaste off our fingers, to cover our breath, and ducked back around the building and into the shower. I felt a little foolish about all the cloak and dagger work for several puffs of smoke but I also felt good that we had outwitted the system and established a tiny bit of independence in the process.

By the time we returned to platoon street I had already forgotten about the incident.

Sgt. Miller, who was on duty that night, stood in front of the formation with a scowl on his face. "Well, well, well, so we have a scumbag in this platoon who doesn't like to follow the same rules as everybody else. Gimme the asshole who snuck around the back of the head for a smoke."

I was thunderstruck. How could he possibly know? I didn't dare move and yet I knew it would be far worse if he found out who it was and I hadn't owned up to it. I looked at Scriver out of the corner of my eye and he looked innocent as a lamb. I could feel the outrage of the platoon. That someone would sneak a smoke and get the lamp put out for everyone was unacceptable. I was about to own up to the deed when Sgt. Miller yelled, "On your faces!" It was too late.

The DI worked on us for half an hour. Finally, his anger in full bloom, he told us to go in the huts and get our rifles. When we returned he made us lay the rifles across the back of our hands and hold our arms straight out. Cries of anguish were heard that night on platoon street.

I could stand it no longer. Realizing that the DI was not going to quit until sunrise, I admitted it.

"Sir, it was me!" I shouted. Platoon 211 hated my guts at that moment.

The drill instructor dismissed the platoon and took me in his hut. Sgt. Miller looked at me and said, "O'Brian, you are the most cowardly, low-down snake I have ever met. I'm washing my hands of you. Tomorrow morning I'm going to personally march you to the brig and personally lock you up. We don't need your kind in this marine corps and I'm going to see to it that you are given an undesirable discharge. You'd better get out of here before I do something that I shouldn't."

I went to bed crushed. We had learned that an undesirable discharge meant that a person would never get a decent job, he would have to register with the FBI every place he went, and in general, he was ruined.

I was still awake ten minutes later when Sgt. Miller's voice rang out, "Platoon 211 on platoon street."

We hustled out on platoon street in our shower shoes and pants and lined up.

"Private O'Brian, front and center."

Oh no—now what?!! I ran·up and reported.

Sgt. Miller smiled at me. "Listen up turds. A private just came to me and told me that there were two smokers in back of the head and not just one. This private, whom I will not name, said that he spotted the smokers and was not going to say anything about it until he saw that Private O'Brian was taking the blame for someone else. The original report that I got said only that there was a cigarette glow behind the head. Now I have an eyewitness

41

report. The people who were smoking were not members of this platoon."

I was really confused now.

"I hope you have learned a lesson tonight. Private O'Brian has just shown you the mark of a good marine. He was willing to sacrifice himself to save the rest of you assholes a night's sleep and a lot of pain and strain. He was not smoking and I know this because the eyewitness saw him going into the head. It would behoove you to remember unselfishness of this nature when and if you are ever in combat."

I couldn't believe it!

"Platoon 211 dismissed."

We went back into the huts and got into bed. Just before the lights went out I craned my neck to look at Gary Scriver. He broke his poker-faced expression for a fraction of a second, winked, and reassumed his deadpan look.

The lights went out and, just as usual, I was asleep in seconds.

CHAPTER FIVE

"It was much pleasanter at home," thought poor Alice, "when one wasn't always growing larger and smaller, and being ordered about by mice and rabbits. I almost wish I hadn't gone down that rabbit-hole—and yet—it's rather curious, you know, this sort of life! I do wonder what can have happened to me! When I used to read fairy tales, I fancied that kind of thing never happened, and now here I am in the middle of one! There ought to be a book written about me, that there ought. And when I grow up, I'll write one—but I'm grown up now," she added in a sorrowful tone: "at least there's no room to grow up any more here." "But then," thought Alice, "shall I never get any older than I am now?..."

Private Johnson returned to the platoon at the end of the second week subdued but still alive. I was curious about what had happened to him during his misadventure and resolved to query him at the very first opportunity.

That night, after mail call, I buttonholed him and said, "John, what the hell went on?"

He looked around quickly, and satisfied that he was not within earshot of any known "snitches," he whispered, "They sent me to the goddam fat farm!"

"What for?"

"Fuckin' PT, man," he groaned. "Physical fuckin' therapy!"

The fat farm had two main functions. The first was to melt fat off overweight recruits and the second was to discipline the trans-gressors of boot camp law and order. The recruits that were too much bother for the DIs to handle at platoon level, yet weren't bad enough to send to the brig, were temporarily assigned to the farm, or "Motivation Platoon." The entire day was spent on physical therapy. Ten-mile runs, calisthenics, obstacle courses, and weight lifting were the only things that were done during the daylight hours. The evenings were devoted to Marine Corps history and games like ping-pong, pool and basketball. The smoking lamp was always lit in the evening and the harassment and threats were kept to a bare minimum.

When the recruits reached an acceptable level of health or motivation they were released and either sent back to their original outfit, or, if too much time had elapsed, to a new unit.

The fat farm did not sound like a bad place to be except that the time didn't count. The actual recruit training had to be done sooner or later and the sooner a person got back to his platoon the quicker he would be graduated from MCRD. Also a private could not simply keep going back every time he got fed up with training. One never knew whether an offense would land him in the brig or the farm, but one thing was certain: the DIs had seen it all and it was very difficult to fool them.

Glen Parker, a natural comic, had come from Motivation Platoon. As a result of a bout with pneumonia and many weeks losing weight, he had been in basic training for a total of six months by the time he was shipped over to 211. I had been there two weeks and it felt like ten years, so I understood what six months meant.

When I got to know Parker I found that he had at least two outstanding qualities. He had learned to endure and he was amazingly unhostile.

One of the foundations of the western way of life is that the fast survive and the slow fall by the wayside. Parker told me that he had been slower than most all his life and when he came into the Marine Corps that tendency was magnified to the point where he couldn't cope with the stress. When his health failed as a

44

result, he decided to call bullshit on the entire way of thinking. He called it "getting out of the express lane."

He was still about twenty pounds overweight but he managed to complete whatever task was required of him. He was almost always last and almost always got the DIs heat but he invariably accomplished what he had to. I became more fascinated with the nature of Private Parker with every passing day. Each day he was harassed and singled out for abuse by both the DIs and the "gung ho" recruits, and for a while it seemed almost like a challenge to them to break his spirit. He never got angry, never fought back, never got sullen, and never stopped trying. I wondered just how much punishment he could absorb before he cracked.

What I eventually realized was that Parker was not absorbing anything. He simply did not resist. He let the noise and pressure flow right past him and never gave it a second thought. By some strange quirk the insanity of boot camp had struck a chord deep within his mind that allowed him not only to remain sane, but gave him an almost tangible aura of peace.

Two years later, in March of 1967, Glen Parker was shot in the chest by a Viet Cong sniper. He was lifted out of the jungle by helicopter and given the finest emergency care available anywhere in the world. He lived for nine days.

At the end of the third week we were scheduled to have our first formal inspection. It was to include a rifle inspection, a clothing inspection that was called "junk on the bunk," and a contest with two other platoons in close order drill. Our days were therefore spent in intensive preparation for the big day. We practiced the drill maneuvers over.and over again for hours, pausing only to do push-ups and other punishments when we erred.

I wanted to win the drill competition with my whole heart and soul because I knew that things would be much easier for us if we did. Some of the recruits had the idea that we would be the "best" group if we won the pennant that was being used as a trophy and that we would be proud of ourselves when other platoons saw the tiny flag waving atop the pole that the platoon "guide" carried. I wasn't about to argue the point of motivation with anyone. All I knew for sure was that it would be a long, sleepless night in the sand pits if we failed to win.

Inspection day came around and we were on edge, not knowing what to expect and very much aware that we were to be inspected by a Marine Corps officer. We had fantasies that a real live officer was a superhuman entity.

We laid out our clothing first thing in the morning and re-cleaned, repolished, reshined, and rechecked everything several times while waiting for the Lieutenant to show up. By the time he arrived I was so nervous that I almost threw up.

We stood in formation while the Lt. looked over our clothing display and checked out the huts and grounds for cleanliness and order.

"Tensh-huuut!" I snapped to, my eyes riveted to the front and my body straight as a ramrod, alert for anything that might come my way. The inspecting officer, Lt. Handall, was saluted by Sgt. Barton and the inspection was underway.

He moved down the line one by one. I could hear each private bring his rifle to the ready and click open the bolt, then the loud snap as the Lt. slapped it out of the recruit's hands. Each private was asked a question as the officer looked over the weapon, then with a flourish, spun it around and handed it back. I could see the movement but as of yet had not laid eyes on the Lt.'s face.

It was my turn. When Lt. Handall stepped in front of me I almost lost control. I came within a whisker of laughing in his face. This man, whom I had fantasized as superhuman, was a skinny, pale, homely looking little person who looked eighteen at most and still had teen-age pimples. The very thought of this guy being a powerful figure, a commander of men, was hilarious. He was the sort of person who should have been at a college fraternity party enjoying a beer with the boys instead of standing out on the drill field acting like General MacArthur.

I imagined that I could see into his mind. He believed with absolute sincerity that he was a man's man, a strong, unbending disciplinarian following in the great tradition of George Wash-

ington, Stonewall Jackson, and U.S. Grant. His hours of boyhood battles with plastic soldiers and cap guns were coexisting
with the present. I wondered what the other career military men
were doing mentally but gave up that line of thought because I
was afraid of the answer.

The Lt. whirled my rifle around with the appropriate non-
chalance, peered down the bore, showed me an imaginary speck
of dirt, whipped it back around, and handed it to me. He gave me
a steely-eyed look with just the right amount of boredom and
scrutiny in it, did a right face and moved on. I had passed. Lt.
Handall hadn't.

After the rifle inspection the close order drill competition
began. We were put through our paces by Sgt. Barton and managed to do each required action with a fair amount of precision
and grace. When the opening jitters wore off we grew stronger
and more confident with each pass and ended our act with a com-
plicated set of turns and reverses that we had practiced many
times without doing it right once. This time it worked as it was
supposed to, and we ended off at that point.

The platoon commander marched us back to our platoon
street where we broke down our rifles and cleaned whatever was
noticed in the inspection. After that we shined and polished some
more while the DIs held a conference with the judges.

We didn't have any idea how the other platoons had done so
we were on pins and needles waiting for the official scores to be
tabulated and for Sgt. Barton to relay the information to us.

Sgt. Barton stepped out of the duty hut. It was impossible to
tell whether we were sinners or saints.

"The smoking lamp is lit for one cigarette," he intoned. A
thundering cheer broke out on platoon street. We had won.

We were preparing to move to Camp Pendleton for training in
rifle marksmanship and the emphasis that the instructors had
been placing on marching was transferred to the M-14 rifle.

We huddled on the floor of a vacant quonset hut while Sgt.
Miller explained the function and importance of our weapons
to us.

47

"This is a marine's best friend," he said, "Take care of it and it'll fuckin' well take care of you."

Private Royce, a lanky mountain boy from Arkansas, stood up and requested permission to speak. It had taken Royce three weeks to learn how to drawl loudly and he had been speaking up quite a bit in the previous couple of days, as if to show that he had indeed caught on. Sgt. Miller was irritated by the interruption.

"Whadda you want Royce, you big, dumb bowl of puke?"

"Suh, Private Royce requests puhmission ta make a haid call?"

"Don't you piss when everybody pisses, sweetheart?"

"Yes, suh, but ah got to take a shet, suh."

"A shet. You goddam beanpole. People don't shet, they shit."

"Yes, suh."

"Is shet past tense, boy, or what?"

There were a few snickers in the small room.

"Suh, the private's feelin' a mite tense, suh, but only cause ah got ta crap real bad." We all laughed at Royce, openly now, including the DI, who was shaking his head in wonderment.

Royce was red with the strain put on his bowels coupled with the strain on his mind in dealing with the Sgt.'s questions. His face was a combination of pain and confusion.

A weird gleam came to the DI's eye as an idea took hold. It looked to me that he was enjoying the situation in a cruel way, much like a child teasing a small animal.

"Well, shitbird," he said with a tight smile, "if you gotta shit you just go right ahead and shit."

"Aye, aye, suh." Royce made a beeline for the door.

"Where do you think you're going, private?" the DI boomed.

"Suh, to the haid."

"I didn't tell you to go to the head, you idiot fuck, I told you to go ahead and take a shit!"

Recognition dawned slowly on Royce's face. He looked as if he was going to start crying.

"Heah, suh?"

"Right here."

He shuffled, blinked, and in a cracked voice whimpered, "Suh, I cain't shet heah."

48

"Is that what you're gonna say in combat, faggot—I can't?"
Royce was crying quietly.

"Start shittin', boy, right fuckin' now!"

The recruit stiffened slightly, then made up his mind and squatted. With a mixture of shame and relief he let the diarrhea pour from his body into his trousers. We broke up. We did not bear malice toward our fellow pvt. But we couldn't hold back our laughter.

"Go clean yourself up turd."

"Aye, aye, suh."

"Since it's an emergency, I want you to sound the siren on the way to the head."

"Aye, aye, suh."

We heard the sound of the southern private's voice simulating a fire engine all the way to the head.

"Now like I say, take good care of this rifle and it'll fuckin' well take good care of you."...

Dear Mom and Dad,

Everything is going really well here in boot camp. We will be leaving for Camp Pendleton tomorrow to go to the rifle range and learn how to shoot our M-14s.

I'm getting in real good shape and enjoy the exercise a lot. The chow is super and we can take as much as we want as long as we eat all we take.

Our DIs are great at training us and I hope to be as squared away as them some day.

The weather is perfect. A guy couldn't ask for a better climate.

This training is rough but I guess that's what it takes to be a Marine.

Well, I hope everything is ok back there in Mpls. and everyone is in good health. Say hello to all the family.

Love,
Danny

Quang Tri Province
Dec. 1965

Our base camp was set up on a hill overlooking a thick patch of jungle. We spent three days making the area as secure as possible. We set up wire, claymores, listening posts, and comm lines in a systematic, thorough fashion.

In the middle of the night, Charlie hit us with everything he had. Round after round of screaming mortars came tearing into the compound, exploding the ear-splitting fury and ripping everything in their path with red-hot chunks of jagged shrapnel. We burrowed into the ground to avoid being hit and hugged mother earth.

When the first barrage had let up Sgt. Slater, the Comm Chief, ran over and jumped into my hole. "O'Brian," he said, "we've lost contact with the listening post on the left flank. I've sent every one of my wiremen out on different assignments and I need somebody to get out there and fix the wire or we're gonna lose those guys. You're volunteering to go."

I looked at the crazy bastard and insisted that I was not volunteering for anything except to get the fuck out of that miserable country. Slater did not find my refusal to volunteer acceptable and told me that I was under orders to get out of my neat little bunker and go fix the line.

Despite a strong urge to spit in his face I got up and strapped on a wireman's belt. I gave the Sgt. my most scathing glance and started off.

"O'Brian!" he yelled. I went back and flopped down. "Take your bayonet—there might be a small mine field at the base of the hill." I grabbed the bayonet and left.

Getting to the listening post was easy. There were flares high in the air that lit up the ground like giant floodlights. The flares had a knack of casting shadows over every piece of vegetation and making them look like gooks lurking in the bush. I went straight east toward the post and when I got to the bottom of the hill on

50

the near side of my destination I dropped to my knees and began poking the bayonet in the ground at an angle to feel for mines.

It seemed highly unlikely that even a small mine field was planted in the area so I wasn't particularly careful about my search. I was much more afraid of being caught in the open by a mortar or a stray round from an AK-47. I got part of the way up the hill and packed away the bayonet. I followed the wire hand-over-hand over the top of the rise and part way downhill until I was close enough to the hole for the guys to hear me. Their orders were to open fire if threatened, and if not in danger, they were to keep quiet.

I said, in a low voice, that I was coming in to check their field telephone and not to shoot. I came to the edge of the well-hidden hole and looked into the barrel of Quinn's newly issued M-16. We both breathed a sigh of relief and I jumped in the hole. The telephone had a loose post, which I repaired. I called in to the CP and told them I was coming back. For some reason I hesitated, then said I would be going back by way of the small road that was cut for jeeps.

By this time it was quiet and the trip back to the CP was uneventful. I found a spot and went to sleep.

In the morning I found my friend, Cpl. Buck, and asked him about the mine setup by the east flank listening post. I explained that I went out there the night before to check a wire because the guys in the hole were cut off and could have been in a bad way.

Buck said, "You're lucky to be here this morning."

I asked why and he explained that Charlie had come in the day after the post had been established and mined the shit out of the area at the base of the hill. Rather than send the men out to dig them up, risking lives and wasting energy, the CO had merely passed the word that the area was off limits and that the road should be used instead of the short-cut.

"You mean it's not just a small mine field?"

"Fuck no," he said, "that sonofabitch is really fuckin' loaded with bettys."

To my mind, Sgt. Slater had deliberately sent me into a field loaded with bouncing bettys, without warning and with malice aforethought. I decided not to confront him with it but to simply wait for his next move.

He was shipped back to the world within the month—in an aluminum box covered by the stars and stripes. Like we used to say, time and time again, "payback is a motherfucker!"

CHAPTER SIX

All in the golden afternoon
Full leisurely we glide;
For both our oars, with little skill,
By little arms are plied,
While little hands make vain pretence
Our wanderings to guide.

The bus pulled off the highway, passed through some gates and proceeded down a bumpy dirt road that eventually wound its way to the ocean. A hundred yards from the beach the bus stopped and we disembarked. We got our heavy seabags from the storage compartment, slung our rifles over our shoulders, and got into formation.

Sgt. Liebermann marched us down to the beach and I saw and heard and smelled the ocean for the first time in my life. The striking beauty and raw power of it impressed me tremendously.

The DIs gave the order to march. From the moment I took the first step and sunk into the sand I knew we were in big trouble. The seabags that we carried weighed about fifty pounds and were awkward to handle under any circumstances but marching in sand with them was doubly difficult. We weren't told how far away the barracks were or how long the forced march would take. We did know that the pain started within fifty yards and would only end when we stopped walking.

The distance turned out to be slightly over five miles and it took us two hours to cover it. Each step seemed as if it would be the last one I could possibly manage. It was far and away the most brutally punishing task that we had been confronted with up to that time in training, and for most of us it was the most difficult physical thing we had faced in our entire lives. Somehow we made it to San Onofre very much the worse for wear.

We were assigned bunks and given a brief introduction to the area where we were to stay for that phase of training and then we fell out in front of the two story barracks.

Sgt. Liebermann led us to the top of a small rise so that we could view the area and become acquainted with it. He pointed out two hills that were so steep they were almost straight up. One was half again as high as the other. Both hills were rubbed bald by exercising recruits of platoons that preceded us.

"Ok, numbnuts, listen up. I want you to take a close look at our main attraction here at scenic San Onofre. The hill on your left is called "Little Agony." The one next to it is known as "Big Agony." We will see to it that you become very familiar with both places and that you come to understand the significance of their names. We feel that since we are your hosts it's the least we can do for you."

I could only wince.

The first morning at the rifle range gave us a wonderful surprise. Sgt. Miller, the junior drill instructor, was no longer with Platoon 211. He had been replaced by a Mexican DI named Cpl. Torres.

I was personally pleased to find that Sgt. Miller would no longer be around to spill his particular brand of poison into our minds. I viewed him as the executioner. Sgt. Barton was the quiet but firm type and Sgt. Liebermann was the storybook marine, mean but fair. Sgt. Miller was simply a vicious man. He was capable of losing control and injuring someone seriously, so having him gone buoyed our morale.

All of the DIs were racists but Sgt. Miller was the most pronounced hatemonger of the three. According to Miller blacks were splibs, niggers, coons, or plain old black cocksuckers. All nonblack recruits were to refer to them as splibs so that there was no racial prejudice. The blacks themselves were to refer to each other as splibs. Italians were greaseball dagos, Mexicans were wetbacks, and jews were kikes. Of course everybody, bar none, was an asshole and a steaming turd so, in the final analysis, we were all equal.

Cpl. Torres seemed rather dull and acted as though he was merely putting in his time. He was not as involved in his work as the other DIs and subsequently wasn't very good at it which was definitely an advantage to us.

On the second day the platoon commander apparently decided that we had had enough orientation because we spent the entire day doing special exercises with the rifle. The drills were intended to make our bodies supple enough to get into the shooting positions and hold those positions for a long time. It was called "snapping in" and was the main thing that we were going to be doing for three weeks.

There were four basic positions: standing, sitting, kneeling, and prone. Each of these positions was designed in such a way that one's rifle would hardly quiver even in gale force winds. By winding the sling in a certain way and contorting the arms and legs a recruit was assured of a fair degree of accuracy in shooting. The price that had to be paid to gain the mastery of the positions was very costly in terms of physical pain and effort and the DIs spared no energy in getting us broken in.

Eleven hours after we started snapping in the DIs called a halt for evening meal. As we were sidestepping through the line to get our food I was talking quietly and laughing with Private Johnson. We ate our meal and marched back to the barracks.

Instead of the expected cigarette break Sgt. Barton called for Pvt. Johnson and me to step forward. I knew then that we had done something wrong but couldn't think of what it could possibly be.

"So you two screws think it's ok to giggle in the fuckin' chow line, eh. I've goddam near had it with both of you. I just might take you out back and unscrew your empty fuckin' heads." He

55

looked us up and down. "Then you know what I'm gonna do?" he snarled, "I'm gonna puke in them and screw 'em back on!"

We were going to be doing extra duty of some kind, that much I knew for sure.

"You two ladies face each other and show me how you laugh."

Johnson and I turned to face each other and forced a laugh, then stopped.

"Keep laughing, idiots."

We made ourselves laugh for several minutes and suddenly, without warning, it became hilariously funny.

There we were, two nearly grown men, standing at attention and laughing in each others faces without pause.

We went in streaks, laughing mechanically for a while and then laughing because it was sincerely funny.

The sun sank slowly in the west and was replaced by the moon. Our platoon as well as the others in various stages of training did their routines and went to bed. We laughed.

All the lights on the base were out and we were still laughing.

Sentries were posted. We laughed and laughed.

My legs turned to lead and my arms hung like weights from my shoulder sockets. My ribs and stomach muscles were on fire. Laughing. My spine had shooting pains and deep inside my belly the organs were turning into mush. Laugh, laugh, I truly thought I would die.

I had never even conceived of an aching tongue. Not ten people on this earth have put such an enormous burden on their precious tongues. I was convinced beyond measure that the tongue is the most vulnerable part of the human anatomy in terms of intensity of ache.

Mercifully, Sgt. Barton came paddling outside in his skivvy shorts and ordered us to go to bed.

It took three days for my tongue to recover. The only time my mouth was ever open in the mess hall after that was when the fork was six inches away and heading home with the payload.

We were assigned a marksmanship instructor named Staff Sgt. Black who was almost fanatical about making bullseyes. At the start of each day he would give us the formula for success in shooting accurately.

He would say in his special monotone, "Let the bull rest halfway up and halfway across your peepsight, take a deep breath, hold, and squeeze the trigger." We were shown diagrams of a correct sighting and had the instructions repeated to us dozens of times every day.

One of the recruits from Oklahoma, a Private Daltry, had apparently failed to assimilate the information even after hundreds of repeated instructions. He scored miserably low on the first day of live fire.

Sgt. Black called Pvt. Daltry to him and asked why he had received such a low score. "What the fuck does this shit represent, swine?"

"Sir, I don't know," Daltry said.

"Did you pay attention to me when I was instructing you, boy?"

"Yes, sir."

"Tell me what a perfect sight looks like."

"Sir, I can't explain it," Private Daltry lied.

Sgt. Black gave the recruit a picture showing the circle of the peepsight lined up with the bull which was resting on the front sight. It was the same picture we had seen so many times before. The instructor walked over to the side of the bleachers and drew a circle with his foot that was about three feet across.

"Now, you dumb okie cluck, I want you to dig a perfect sight picture right here. Dig it deep. If you fuck me up on qualification day I'm gonna hang you by your nuts. Understand?"

"Yes, sir."

The ground was made up of hard clay that would have been difficult to dig with a shovel and Daltry was faced with the prospect of digging into it with his bare hands. He scratched feebly at the spot for a few minutes until finally the Sgt. exploded. He ran to the area and gave a mighty swing of his foot, kicked the private square in the ass and sent him tumbling.

"I said dig!" he screamed, veins standing out like clotheslines in his thick neck.

For the rest of the week Private Daltry worked with broken and bleeding fingernails on the sight picture for at least two hours each day. By the time the instructor let him go he had learned beyond question how to sight in his rifle.

The second week on the rifle range found us undergoing a subtle but significant change. The pressure to qualify with a high enough score was greatly increased but somehow the source of the pressure had changed from the DIs to the platoon members themselves. The instructors still played a large role in that they set the tempo of our daily routine and kept our minds channeled in the required direction. Without our awareness however, they had designated several privates as unnamed "leaders" in the bid to have the entire platoon demonstrate the necessary skills on "qual" day.

Private Garden, a small, cocky man from Denver, became the number one motivator. He worked at a zealous pace during the days on the range, spent his thirty-minute free period in the evening dry firing his rifle and doing extra calisthenics, and harassed and harangued anyone he felt was not working up to capacity. In general he made himself very visible and very obnoxious.

Private Jones had a difficult time from the first day of boot camp and the marksmanship training proved to be no exception. He was the smallest recruit in the group, which did him little good as far as physical stamina was concerned and was positively disastrous when it came time for the natural sharks to define the pecking order of the group. In short order he became Pvt. Garden's favorite target.

One day, which had been particularly bad for Jones, was especially good for Garden. He had shot in the expert range while Jones floundered about in the failing category. We returned from the range and were cleaning our weapons when Garden hissed, "Jones, you little mother fucker, why don't you straighten up and fly right?"

Private Jones continued to look down at his rifle.

"Keep fuckin' up man and I'm gonna make you one sorry

sumbitch. We don't need nobody draggin' us down so you best wake up in a hurry."

Jones looked up, visibly upset. "Hey, I'm trying my best. Why don't you get off my back?"

Garden smelled blood. "I'll stay all over you shitbird, till I think you can do the job like the rest of us. Remember, I'm right behind you every fuckin' day." He had a strange look of righteous anger and pleasure on his face. He thought he was a DI.

It was becoming obvious that the training was "taking." The platoon members were losing whatever resistance there was originally and were slowly shifting over to the "other side." Most of the recruits in the group had willingly assumed the identities of fawning, slave-like people. I, and the several people I knew who were resisting the process, were also obedient machines, but under the surface we held onto a spark of self-determinism and nurtured the hope that we would endure the indoctrination with the core of our own identities intact.

Our appetites for food had grown to enormous proportions and every scrap that was put on the steel trays was efficiently consumed. Someone started a food fad. We would take a piece of white bread, spread butter on it, and then load it down with a quarter inch of sugar and eat it for dessert. I often thought that it would cause a normal person to gag but we considered it a delicious treat.

Another thing that gave us pleasure was an after-meal cigarette. We had gotten into the habit of getting up, going to breakfast, marching to the range with precision and spirit, climbing into the bleachers, and waiting for the smoking lamp to be lit. It always was.

One morning we went through the normal routine, everything clicking as usual. We got into the bleachers and waited for the ok to light up. It was not forthcoming.

Cpl. Torres, the Mexican DI, told us we were fucks and to fall in with our rifles. I didn't understand what the problem was.

The DI screamed and fumed as he worked us over. Something had really set him off and none of us had any idea what it was.

We had done everything with vigor and precision and in all fairness we should have been sitting down relaxing and waiting for the rifle instructor to show up.

I could feel myself panic as I realized that Torres was not himself at that moment. The irrationality of his actions made something happen to me that I couldn't control.

"One-two-three-four, get your fuckeeng hands up, girls!"

We were exercising rather than smoking.

"Move it, pukey ladies...one-two..."

No fucking cigarette!!

"On your faces, sheetheads..one-two-three-four...."

You dirty Mexican fucker!!!

"One-two...on your feet, hogs!"

You dirty fucking animal Mexican bastard!!!!! God give me a bullet—just one bullet for one second so I can blow him off the earth. Jesus please let me kill him, God please, please let me shoot this evil bastard dead!!

"Quickly, ladies, quickly, on your backs!" One-two-...."

There was no doubt in my mind that I would have shot and killed the man there on the spot if I had a live bullet. Never had I been so enraged at another human being that I wanted to deliberately take his life but I would have gleefully snuffed out the DI no matter what the consequences were.

In less than thirty-five days I had acquired the potential to deliberately and willingly slay another man. We had come a long way in a short time.

On the Sunday before our last week on the rifle range we were allowed to purchase a newspaper and read it while we sat on our ever-present buckets in front of the barracks.

To me it was like a drink of cold water after a month in the desert. I slowly, almost tenderly, worked my way through the comics, then the sports section, and finally, to the world news.

MARINES LAND IN DANANG!

I flew through the article. 3,500 marines of the 9th Marine Expeditionary Brigade had waded ashore in the port city of Da Nang, South Vietnam. Casualties were described as light.

A perimeter had been formed and reinforcements were expected shortly.

I had heard news of American advisors in Viet Nam and read infrequently of an American being killed so there was some familiarity with it. There was a lot of difference, though, between a handful of advisors and 3,500 marines. I could sense that something of magnitude was going to occur even though the reality of the next few years greatly exceeded my original view.

A buzz of excitement ran through 211 as the news traveled that we were at war. The air was charged as privates talked about how they were going to kick ass on the fuckin' slanteyes.

Private Garden allowed as to how we'd better learn to shoot our piece straight or some zipperhead would likely blow us away.

Private Johnson decided he'd stack up a shit load of medals to show his kids.

Private Scott figured his older brother had already bagged a few gooks for old glory.

There was general agreement that Viet Nam was what we were all working so hard for and and all the training would be worthwhile when some dink came around and we'd finally have a chance to score.

I tried to feel happy about it but it just didn't work. I knew good and well that I did not want to go off to some disease-ridden jungle and live like an animal while I hunted down some other animal for the sole purpose of killing him or being killed. Even so I joined the brave conversation and added my bit to it.

That evening Sgt. Liebermann gathered us in front of his office and gave us a short talk about our future.

"This is what we've been waiting for girls," he said, "twelve years we've been waiting for the enemy to rear his ugly head. Twelve long years the Corps has been without a good shootin' war and not it looks like we've finally got one. You sweethearts had best keep your eyes and ears open and your mouths shut cause you're gonna have your young asses in combat before you know it. When you fuck up in combat, turds, you get killed. Make a mistake in the bush and some gook fucker is like to knock your dick stiff. Mind my words, ladies. The United States Marine Corps has been kickin' the ass end off've our enemies for well on two hundred years and we plan to go on kickin' ass for two hundred more. We've been hoping since Korea for another shot at the slopeheads, so you maggots master your weapons here and now while you got yourselves a chance because there ain't no second chance when the shit hits the fan. Just bear in mind this one thing: so far it's not much of a war but it's a damn sight better than no war at all." He paused, his eyes shining with pride. "The smoking lamp's lit for one."

"Sir, the smoking lamp's lit for one, aye, aye, sir!" Celebration on platoon street! War was at hand and with war came glory. Mourning could wait because tonight the lamp was lit and the bravery and excitement of two hundred years was once again reborn. Its renewed life unleashed a powerful and primitive instinct in us that was undeniable.

March 12, 1965

Dear Mom and Dad,

I hope everything is just fine back home there in the North Country. It was real nice to hear from you and I hope that you'll keep writing often.

We're getting ready to qualify on the range now and I figure I'm a real good marksman. I can hit about eight bullseyes out of ten shots from five hundred yards. You won't find very many people in the other branches of service who can do that well because they just don't have the training that we do.

I've been thinking of making a career out of the Marines and I'll need to be a good shot for sure if I'm in for twenty years. At least I know I'd hate to come face to face with a gook and have him be the better shot. Ha! Ha!

To be serious for a minute, I'm almost a Marine now and the training that we're getting really proves to me why the marines are the best fighting men in the world. Of course it's not a tea party. We're learning

62

the things that we have to know in order to make it in combat and some of it ain't exactly what you call pretty. But that's what it takes to be a man and that's what it takes to be able to wear the proudest uniform in the world.

I suppose by now you've heard of the war in South Vietnam. I guess the commies are trying to overthrow the democracy and we have to stop it 'cause Russia and China are behind it all. If we don't stop communism now we'll be fighting in our own back yards pretty soon. I don't know what the particulars are but I figure that President Johnson does and that's good enough for me. I may die, but at least I'll die fighting for what I know is right.

That's enough seriousness. Say hello to everyone for me and let the family know that I'm doing real good.

Love to All,
Danny

CHAPTER SEVEN

"Speak roughly to your little boy,
And beat him when he sneezes;
He only does it to annoy,
Because he knows it teases."

"I speak severly to my boy,
I beat him when he sneezes;
For he can thoroughly enjoy
The pepper when he pleases!"

The final week of training at the rifle range found us stepping
up the pace in our race to acquire the skills necessary for qualification with the M-14. The mornings were devoted mainly to
dry fire practice and the afternoons to classes and live firing.
In the evenings we fine-tuned our bodies with long, fast runs
and calisthenics. Our physical condition had improved so much
from the time we first started training that it was truly amazing.

We shifted psychological gears again during "qual week."
The DIs backed off even further than they had in the previous
week and the constant state of scrutiny by them was lifted. We
still maintained a carefully plotted schedule every day and no
noise or blatant individuality was allowed, but the instructors
permitted us a bit looser rein when it came to chatting quietly
or eating more slowly or buying personal articles in the post

exchange such as razor blades or soap. We were allowed to choose our own brand names, take seconds in the chow line, talk in the evening for thirty minutes instead of writing home or shining our gear, and so on. The cursing and screaming came to a near standstill and only when a flagrant violation of camp rules occurred did a DI step in to administer punishment They even smiled and joked with us occasionally!

The situation was more acceptable during that week than it had been at any point up until then and it even seemed like a fairly pleasant place to be at times. The instructors were giving us their unspoken consent to relax. I started the week thinking that because we were now semicompetent and well along in our training that the DIs were beginning to respect us and wanted to show us that. I hadn't actually stopped to consider that we had live bullets during the day for one thing and, for another, that we would be at a disadvantage when it came to shoot if we were tense.

At any rate, I was too thankful to question the change of attitude very closely. I just hoped that we could win another pennant and keep the tolerance of the DIs at that level.

The week had finally run its course. Because of the combination of hard work, exercise, deep sleep, and good food we were in tip-top physical condition. The lifting of the chronic pressure to do everything just right had left us in a frame of mind where we could concentrate solely on our marksmanship. We were relaxed and ready.

On Thursday night we had light calisthenics, took good hot showers and hit the rack at the normal 8:30. The lights went out and silence fell over the squad bay.

A couple of minutes after lights out Sgt. Barton came out of his office and began walking around the barracks, speaking to us in a mellow, almost gentle voice. Never had he seemed so much like the Forgiving Father than he did at that moment.

"Well, girls," he began, "We've come a long way from the first day of training. Six weeks ago you were a bunch of raggedy-assed civilians who couldn't put one foot in front of the other.

We've all worked hard and now we've reached the most important day in your quest to become marines."

"I want you to remember that every marine, regardless of his rank or job is first and foremost a rifleman. Many, many times cooks and bakers and supply men and truckdrivers have been called on to go into combat at a moment's notice. It's not just the infantryman that must have a mastery of his weapon. In one hundred and ninety years there has never been a marine who wasn't trained for combat."

"When you get on the firing line tomorrow I want you to think before each and every shot you fire. Check your windage and elevation. Mark down every shot so that you'll know which way to adjust if it becomes necessary. You've worked too damned hard to fuck up because of carelessness. Relax and take your time. Make sure you're lined up on the right target, sight in with a perfect sight picture, take a deep breath, hold, and squeeze the trigger. On your rapid fire squeeze the trigger, don't jerk it. If you use your heads you will qualify."

"This is the only chance you will get. You are not shooting to please me or anyone else. When you get into combat, and you can almost bet you will, you must be able to shoot your weapon accurately."

"I'll tell you very honestly that the other platoons around here do not match up to you. I expect you to outclass them all tomorrow and bring that pennant home. Just keep in mind what you have learned, use your heads, and everything will come out just fine. Get some sleep now."

I had a lump in my throat realizing what a fine, decent man Sgt. Barton really was. He really hadn't been degrading and hurting us at all. His real purpose was to see us learn how to survive in war and he actually cared for us very deeply. He had shown us his true self and we were moved. The last sounds I heard as I fell asleep were a few embarrassed coughs.

Qual day broke clear and cool with no wind. Perfect!
We were in a state of controlled tension as we went through

our usual morning procedure of shaving, breakfast, and brisk march to the firing range. Although the things we were doing were routine, we were very much aware that it was a special day, maybe the most special day of our lives thus far.

To an outsider it might have looked as though we were merely doing what we had done every other day so far but the fact was that for the vast majority of recruits there had never been a personal experience quite like it. In most enterprises one either succeeds or doesn't and either way it simply does not make that great a difference in one's life. With this test one either succeeded and was "normal" or failed and was the most miserable wretch imaginable. The idea of not passing the test of marksmanship was so horrible that it could not be comprehended by someone who hadn't personally experienced it. To fail was not merely a tribute to one's incompetence. It was an absolute betrayal of oneself, the platoon, the DIs, the history and tradition of the Marine Corps and, indeed, all freedom-loving people everywhere. The enormity of failure in this case was, of course, not sane but nevertheless was very real.

On the other hand, the many hours of drilling, the constant repetition of instructions, and the uncompromising mental discipline had instilled a kind of certainty in us all that we would, in the final analysis, qualify as marine marksmen.

We started at the two-hundred-yard line in the standing position. Very careful of my technique, I methodically worked through all ten shots and made a respectable showing. Then we went into rapid fire drill in the sitting position. Nothing drastic happened and I knew I was going to pass. It began to feel very anticlimatic. We moved back to the three hundred-yard line for slow fire sitting and kneeling and rapid fire prone. I shot average and from what I could observe all the other privates in 211 were doing fine. We finished there and went to the final firing line, five hundred yards.

On the ninth shot at five hundred yards I missed the target completely. I was surprised to see the red rag waved slowly across my target by the recruits keeping score in the target pit. The only thing I could figure out was that I had aimed in on the wrong target. I decided before taking my final shot that I would recheck my total score for the day. I had calculated that I had already qualified with the required 190 points. I added up only 185. I knew there was some mistake, and I was lost in trying to find it and running out of time in the meanwhile. If I did have only 185 it meant I would need a 5-pt. bullseye on the last shot or it was the end of me. I had been so casual about this thing once the firing started and now I had worked myself into a position whereby anything less than a perfect shot meant doom. I put the bullet in, said a prayer to Jesus and a prayer to the devil so that I would be covered on both ends, and fired. It was a bullseye. Pass. I thanked Jesus and moved off the line.

When the official scorer handed me the card it said 195, the score I had originally figured.

The last man finished and we walked back to platoon street to clean our rifles and wait for the official score to come in. We were ordered to be silent.

The pennant for the rifle range was the most prestigious of all and waiting for the results to filter down to us was like sweating blood.

A deafening cheer broke out in Platoon 212's area and we hung our heads and kept cleaning.

"Private Garden!"

Oh no!! Of all the people in the group it was Garden! I felt a wave of exaltation for a second.

"Sir, Private Garden reporting as ordered, sir."

"Get your maggoty, scummy, rotten little pig's breath up in my office!" barked Sgt. Barton.

A bewildered and broken Private Garden ran into the barracks to the DI's office and we could hear the door slam. Muffled shouts came through the closed door and we knew for sure that Garden was getting an asswhipping, the likes of which he'd probably never known.

We sat in the fading twilight and I could sense a buildup of frustration and anger at our failure to score 100% qualified. Private Garden was the target of the anger and I was silently grateful that it was him in the office and not me.

69

A tightly controlled Sgt. Barton came to the platoon street and through clenched teeth ordered us to put away our rifles. I knew at that instant that the "respect" the DIs had shown us in the previous week had been an act designed for one thing and that was the enhancement of their own records by having us win the marksmanship flag We put away our equipment and returned to the street.

What our failure had actually come down to was a personal insult to the Forgiving Father and his sidekick, Sgt. Liebermann. We had besmirched their records and for that we would pay dearly, with intensity and frequency.

The two DIs got on us that night like never before. We did push-ups, sit-ups, squat thrusts, and rifle exercises. We duck-walked up and down Big and Little Agony. We rolled and groveled and thrashed about until we cried for mercy. Both Sgts. ranted and screamed and kicked their ways up and down the ranks, pouring scalding insults over us for hours.

The night finally ended when loss of control was imminent, not because we refused to obey, but because our bodies would no longer respond no matter what we were threatened with.

Before I fell asleep that night the thought occurred to me that I had lost something valuable—my ability to view at least some of the training with a sense of humor. I could feel an insurmountable wall shutting off that point of view and crushing it right out of existence. Even though I knew humor was an important safety valve there was nothing I could do to save that part of my mind. Five months past the age of seventeen, I felt old and bitter and drained. I very seriously rolled over and went to sleep.

❦ ❦ ❦

Chu Lai, Feb., 1966
After 6 months in the bush the R&R assignments came through. Rest and Relaxation for several days was suppose to prepare one for another few months of stress and boredom in Vietnam.

Tradition has it that the youngest man in the company gets first choice when R&R is picked. Since I was the baby of the family I took the only available opening—three days in Okinawa, air fare paid. It wasn't Hong Kong or Tokyo, but it was a helluva lot better than what I was used to.

I was sent to the airfield at Da Nang to catch a flight out of country. The ride up there in the convoy was uneventful with the exception of a small attack set up by a handful of gooks with a mortar tube and a bent for suicide. They got off a half-dozen ill-aimed rounds before we literally chopped them into chunks with small arms and recoilless rifle fire.

At Da Nang I had a one day wait for my flight so I strapped on my pistol and sauntered into the city to see what I could see. It was torn up from years of fighting but it was the closest thing to civilized living I had seen in some time, so I found it very pleasurable just to wander about aimlessly watching the peasants hawk their meager wares to the lucky soldiers who were assigned to the area on a full-time basis.

A young boy of perhaps six years of age pulled me aside and whispered, "Hey, Joe, you want smoke? You want boom-boom?" Feeling lucky in love and having a lot of time to kill I told the kid that I'd take a little bit of both, whereupon he led me through some back alleys that reeked of filth and were littered with the discarded remnants of the people.

He showed me into a shack made of rotting board and tin and introduced me to a skinny slow-eyed teenager named Lin. The boy took his ten piastre note and made his exit, leaving me alone with the girl.

Lin had shifty eyes which made me paranoid so before ordering one of the small plastic ten-packs of pot I loosened the flap that covered the forty-five on my hip, letting her know that I'd blow her away if anything unusual was on her mind. My own mind was seized with freewheeling pictures of VC slinking around outside waiting for a signal.

She sent a little girl for the marijuana and I was very shortly stoned and grinning. The marijuana was already a way of life with me and it was my most loyal companion, always there,

71

never hesitating to give me a brief escape from the tedious bullshit, and ever willing to be shared with unknown people of the lower ranks. At least 80% of the enlisted men from the rank of Corporal on down smoked it so we had a kind of shared reality regardless of background or future.

The girl asked me if I was ready to boom-boom. Something in her demeanor told me to be careful so I took the gun out and eased a round into the chamber. Her eyes went wide, then relaxed as though she had experienced that small brand of madness many times. She took off her clothes and lay on the canvas cot brushing away the ever-present flies. I took off my pants, leaving my boots and shirt on in case I needed to split in a hurry, and crawled on top of her. She closed her eyes as I hacked away at her body in a loveless, pleasureless rhythm. I hated her degradation, her poverty and her too-skinny body. I also hated her brothers and sisters and aunts and uncles and even her old black-toothed granny.

I reached down to the floor and picked up the loaded .45. I cocked the hammer back and put the yawning barrel to the girl's temple. She opened her eyes and saw that she was going to die with some complete stranger fucking away at her. In a desperate attempt to save her life she started wriggling and babbling in her native tongue. The sudden stimulus caused my body to spurt its load of sperm into her belly. I relaxed the hammer of the gun and put it back on the floor. I disengaged from the girl, put my pants back on, collected my gear, and walked out.

I wandered about the streets for a few minutes feeling like a pervert. I was talking to myself, trying to figure out how things ever got to such a point that I would threaten someone with death out of sheer meanness. I looked around at the filth and greed and desperation of the ragged people hustling and grubbing in the rubble of the ruined city and decided that it didn't make a fucking bit of difference how I acted. There was already more misery here than in any other square mile on earth, so trying to be noble and righteous was not only out of context, it was completely ridiculous. The only thing that the Vietnamese and I had in common was a desire to be left alone and the powers that be were not about to let that happen.

I lit another joint, found a group of blacks hanging out on a corner, lied about how I was from Philly, and was accepted as a white brother. We shared our pot and some Vietnamese whisky until the sun started to go weak and it was time to head back to the compound.

I went to sleep that night drugged to the gills, dreaming about how much fun it would be to go to Okinawa the next day. The women would be soft and beautiful. There would be flushing toilets and cars and lights at night and paved roads. I pretended that it would be meaningful and fulfilling, knowing full well that I was bullshitting myself all the while.

CHAPTER EIGHT

Alice began to feel very uneasy: to be sure, she had not as yet had any dispute with the Queen, but she knew that it might happen any minute, "and then," thought she, "what would become of me? They're dreadfully fond of beheading people here: the great wonder is, that there's anyone left alive!"

She was looking about for some way of escape, and wondering whether she could get away without being seen....

Back in San Diego, the third phase of our training was underway. This was the polishing period and was intended to complete our mental and physical transformation into marines and prepare us for infantry training, which would take place immediately following our successful completion of boot camp.

Complete and unquestioning obedience to orders was now automatic and so more attention was placed on physical fitness, academic knowledge, and awareness of tradition. The browbeating by the drill instructors became a secondary part of our lives. To be sure, there was no letup in the barrage of abuse or in the tightly controlled schedule. The difference was that it had become the normal thing and was no longer as alien and painful as it had been in the beginning. A dog that is beaten everyday is afraid of his master but comes to accept his lot and learns to live with it. He will also continue to eat the food his owner puts out. Even though we were not dogs the situation and results were the same.

We began spending four or five hours every day on the conditioning course. There were walls, ropes, logs, barbed wire, drain pipes, and several other props to use for conditioning the recruits physically.

One of the most difficult obstacles was the water hole. It was a pit of stagnant water that was supposed to be crossed by swinging on a rope suspended from above on a beam. In order to successfully cross the pit the recruit would have to grasp the heavy rope, move as far back as possible, and make a leaping swing across. It was hard but if done properly the crossing could be navigated without getting dunked. The real liability of the drill was that the water was so foul that the stench made us literally gag.

To demonstrate how to cross the water Sgt. Liebermann, standing upwind, took the heaviest private in the platoon and used him to show us what not to do. Glen Parker, for the umpteenth time, was the victim.

"Take this rope, sweetheart," the DI said. He positioned Parker at the edge of the pit. "Now you take 'n' swing your big fat ass out across that lake when I give you the word." The DI moved us in closer and told us to pay attention. He could not quite hide a grin.

"Swing!" he yelled.

Parker arced out over the water and came about three feet from the other side. He tried to swing back to the first side and didn't make it. He swung in smaller and smaller arcs until the rope was hanging uselessly directed above the rotten water. He started to kick his legs to get moving again but gave that up as a futile gesture. The strain of hanging on was showing in his blood-gorged face and his knuckles were white with the pressure. He hung there, turning slowly, for about half a minute. Then he looked at us, let go with one hand and plugged his nose, took a quick breath and, like a sinking ship, slid into the green slime. He surfaced and paddled over to the side, then hauled himself out and wiped the muck from his face.

"That's how not to do it, ladies," the DI said, "so do it right and you won't get your little pussys wet in the lake."

He looked at Parker. "You stink, asshole, go get cleaned up."

"Aye, aye, sir." The overweight private took off at a gallop for the showers.

A monument that honored the genius of the conditioning course engineers was the log ladder. It was a giant structure composed of logs that stood about thirty-feet high and was ten-feet wide. It looked like two huge ladders leaning against each other at forty-five degree angles. The objective was to climb up one side, swing over the top, and climb back down the other side. The catch was that the space between the top rung and the second rung was greater than the average person could reach. Only the tallest privates were spared the thrill of jumping to reach the top rung. When my turn came I climbed easily to the top. My knees were trembling as I looked down three stories and knew I had to jump up to the top of the structure or get smashed by a DI. I stood up, held onto a brace, stretched like never before and jumped up. I caught the top rung and pulled myself up, dangling a leg on each side for balance. Then I had to hang and drop to the second rung and grab the brace at the same time. I swallowed my heart and did it, then scrambled down to the blessed earth and got back in line.

Private Swenson, when it came his turn, went up slowly and carefully, got to the secondmost rung and stopped to rest. He spent an unusually long time contemplating his predicament. Eventually he was ready to move. He stood up stiffly, looked down at the ground, and reassumed his crouched position. He repeated the movement three times and then finally made up his mind. He crawled back down the same way he had gone up.

Sgt. Barton couldn't believe his eyes. A recruit had not gone over the top as ordered! The DIs eyes bulged out and his face turned white.

"Get over here, pigpen!" the Sgt. boomed.

Swenson ran to him and reported as ordered. He was less afraid of the DI than he was of falling three stories.

"You fucking maggot! I don't believe you!" The DI's voice had that high pitch of someone who was completely baffled by the shocking behavior of another. "You mean to show me that you aren't going over that ladder? I'm gonna kick your fucking face in and leave you for dead if you don't get that goddam fuckin' brain of yours right, blue eyes! You get your ass over to the General's grass double-time, swine!"

Swennie ran over to the sand near the edge of the road and stood at attention. The DIs called the sand "grass" and often had us water it with buckets to make it grow. When the "grass" didn't grow we were punished. Of course everything on the base belonged to the Corps, the General, and DIs. Apparently the ownership was interchangeable depending on the mood of the instructor at the time. At any rate Swenson stood by the General's grass for some time.

Sgt. Barton ignored the recruit for awhile, then walked over to him. He cupped his mouth with his hands and yelled with all his strength into Swenson's ear. The command he gave was the most dreaded one of all, "Thrash!"

The private lay down in the sand and started thrashing. The idea of thrashing was to throw oneself into the sand with utter abandon, flopping and wiggling and twisting like a freshly landed pike. Thrashing was a physical and mental disaster. Sand would get inside the clothing and fill every orifice of the body with painful, chafing grit. Along with the discomfort of the sand was the enormous energy expended in a very short time that soon ran out and left one short of breath with very tired muscles and no hope of quitting the exercise.

Swenson was kicking up sand and dust and his tortured grunts could be heard for half a city block.

"Thrash harder, maggot, you ain't moving fast enough!"

The unhappy private tried but was soon out of gas and his thrashing was reduced to a whimpering wiggle.

"Get up, asshole!"

Swennie got to his feet and stood in front of the DI, swaying and covered from head to toe with dust.

"Did you fuck up the General's grass, turd?"

"Yes sir."

"Why did you fuck up the General's grass, scumbag?"

"Sir, I was thrashing, sir."

"Did the General give you permission to fuck up his grass?"

"No, sir."

"You better water that grass, you slimy queer, before the General comes by and sees what you did to it."

"Aye, aye, sir."

Private Swenson ran off to get buckets while the DI gathered us around the grass in a semicircle.

With a full bucket of water in each hand Swennie staggered to the sand pit, paused, and threw the water on the sand. He then turned and ran for refills.

"The smoking lamp is lit for one."

"Sir, the smoking lamp is lit for one, aye, aye, sir."

We sat and watched Private Swenson go back and forth with buckets while we puffed on our cigarettes. They were delicious.

An exercise that we did a lot was logrolling. The drill had two effects on the platoon that were readily noticeable. The first was the building up of strength and stamina.

Under the supervision of a training instructor and on his command we would lift a huge log in teams of five and do various exercises with it. The great weight and bulkiness of the log and the twisting and turning of it added to the physical conditioning of each man assigned to the log.

The more subtle but more important effect of logrolling was the teamwork aspect. Each private had to be responsible for his own section of the log and also for the log as a whole. We had to lift, turn, and spin, in harmony with the other privates or it just wouldn't work. If one private slacked off even slightly the entire effort was thrown out of balance because the weight was distributed in such a way that weakness at one point caused too much weight to shift into the next sector and a chain reaction would start which could, and sometimes did, end up with the log on top of someone's chest.

After working out one morning we were marched in a heavy rainstorm to a warehouse to be measured for dress uniforms.

The significance of getting our formal uniforms was not lost on us because we were all aware that it meant we were on a clear path towards graduation. It was a very unpleasant day to be out marching but we were in high spirits.

There was a snag of some sort in the schedule so when we got to the warehouse the DIs lined us up along the edge of the tin building where we settled in for the wait.

We stood wrapped up in our ponchos for about half an hour when a very curious thing happened. I got an erection. A hard on! Would wonders never cease? For the first time in what seemed like months the pressure had been lifted enough to allow my body to function as a seventeen-year-old body naturally does. I was positively elated! It had not occurred to me in weeks that sexuality was a part of my make-up. I'm sure the experience of raising a hard on at that point was very similar to the happiness a senior citizen must feel when he and grandma join in infrequent intercourse.

It did not take long to come to the conclusion that I had been physically castrated during the process of becoming a man according to the marine definition of the word. The rediscovery of my cock had three separate results. First, it marked the rebirth of my sexual awareness and therefore my humanness. Second, it broke down more of the machinery that had been so ingeniously designed and engineered by the instructors, and third, it brought about my decision to escape.

CHAPTER NINE

"The first thing I've got to do," said Alice to herself, as she wandered about in the wood, "is to grow to my right size again; and the second thing is to find my way into that lovely garden. I think that will be the best plan."

It sounded an excellent plan, no doubt, and very neatly and simply arranged; the only difficulty was, that she had not the smallest idea how to set about it....

I spent the rest of the day plotting my escape and by the time we went to bed I was satisfied that I had a workable plan.

I waited until everyone was asleep and the base was quiet, then put on my clothes and walked quietly out the back door of the quonset hut. It was dark out but the sky had cleared up and it was warm enough so I could not use the weather as an excuse to turn back as my every impulse directed.

I took a breath and headed across the drill field for the barracks on the other side. The barracks housed marines who were permanently assigned to MCRD. I stopped halfway across, turned around, turned around again, and continued on my way. I decided to quit fighting myself and put all my attention on making the escape successful.

I reached the other side and very quietly but boldly walked into the sleeping area of the barracks as if I belonged there. I picked up a sleeping marine's civilian clothes and went back through the hallway to the bathroom. I exchanged pants and shirt, kept my own boots, and walked back outside in my new attire, stopping at the bottom of the stairs to throw my uniform in a garbage can.

I suddenly realized that I did not know my way around the base so I decided to stay on the main streets. I headed for the base theatre which I did know was more or less the center of traffic. I figured one of the roads there would lead to a fence or gate that I could go over. I reached the theatre, picked a street, and followed it. Thinking that boldness was the way to handle it I strode down the street and, miraculously, was not stopped and questioned.

I managed to find my way to a gate. The only trouble was that it was the main gate to the base and was brightly lit and heavily guarded by marines with .45 caliber pistols. I expected to find a peaceful little wall with no one around to stop me from leaving. Reality presented an extremely difficult problem.

I hid in the shadows of a brick building behind some bushes and tried to slow my heart down. I wished mightily that I had stayed in bed where I was put by Sgt. Barton. I was caught no matter what happened. Even if I did go back to the barracks my clothes, with my name and number stencilled on them, were in the GI can at the permanent barracks. I couldn't go back for them because I couldn't remember exactly which barracks I stole the clothes from. I was plainly and simply fucked no matter which way I turned so my only option was to get out the front gate somehow.

I took a coin from my pocket and scratched on the wall: DJ O'Brian RIP. I grinned. Black humor was better than no humor. I was ready to act recklessly. In a dangerous situation where there was no way out the only thing I could think of to do was enjoy the danger.

I pictured Humphrey Bogart escaping from San Quentin in a laundry truck. I thought of Steve McQueen jumping his motorcylcle over a wall in World War II Germany. I couldn't seem to find a connection between real life and my dreams.

I sat in the shadows alternately dozing and plotting. I was tired, cramped, cold, unhappy, and scared. And hungry. If I could only get to the mess hall for some food. The mess hall.

Trucks. The food that we ate had to come from outside the base in trucks. That was it! A food truck!

I got up from my hiding place and wandered around the streets until I got my bearings, then headed for the mess hall.

"Halt!"

I stopped walking.

"Who goes there?"

My mind was a blur. "Corporal Jackson."

"Step forward and identify yourself."

I walked up to the guard and saw that he was a recruit. Good.

"May I see some ID, sir?" he asked.

"Hey, boy, I'm on my way back from the club and I ain't got no fuckin' ID. You wanna fuck with me about it, turd? Your goddam job is to stop fuckin' civilians from walking around my fucking base, not fuck with NCOs."

"Aye, aye, sir."

"Walk your post, private."

"Aye, aye, sir."

I walked off arrogantly. He slunk off like a scolded dog. No wonder the DIs hated us, I thought.

I made it to chow hall and snuck around the back. Sure enough, there were a half dozen trucks in various stages of unloading. I spotted a bread truck that was nearly empty and proceeded to crawl under the loading dock to a spot directly behind it and waited for the job to be finished.

When the truck was emptied the driver shut the sliding door and went inside to get someone to sign for the goods. At that point I crouched and ran to the side door, opened it and slid into the passenger seat. I squeezed my way into the rear area where the food was kept and hunkered down under a shelf of trays to avoid being seen by the driver. He came out, hopped into the driving seat, put the truck in gear, and drove off without so much as a backwards glance. I knew I was out if we could only make the front gate.

My heart was singing as the sentry waved the driver through the gates with a cheerful "Good morning." We hadn't even come to a complete stop.

Things were definitely looking up as that was the first genuinely cheerful human voice that I had heard in two months.

I was on my way.

We drove for about twenty minutes and then the van pulled in some place and rolled to a stop. The driver jockeyed back and forth a few times before cutting the engine. I heard him rustling papers around and finally, finished with his irritating ritual, he opened his door and got out.

I didn't want to wait too long because I figured that someone would be along to clean up the truck so I chanced a quick peek out the front window. There was a bakery about fifty feet to the front with a loading dock attached and populated with perhaps ten men in hard hats. I was puzzled at the hard-hats but was not inclined to ponder the mystery of loading bread in such a uniform. To either side of the well-lit dock the building extended for about fifty feet.

I doubted that the situation would get better so I crawled up front and quietly opened the door and got out. I immediately dropped to the ground for an overall look. Behind me were about thirty vehicles similar to my escape truck and behind them was a retaining wall ten feet high topped with a chain link fence. The back way was completely out of the question.

I got ready and stood up in plain view. I started walking straight towards the loading dock and was spotted right away.

The first man to see me yelled out, "Hey, whadda you doing back there?" I continued to walk nonchalantly directly at the men and hoped that doing so would allay their suspicions, at least for a few moments. My heart was beating wildly and I had a hard time breathing. This was my tightest spot since I left the platoon area.

One of the hard-hats climbed down the steps to meet me and said, "Can I help you with something?" There was definitely a note of hostile suspicion in his voice. I still didn't answer.

I was halfway to the dock and the rest of the men were moving toward the steps, ready to do their part if their hunch proved correct.

I changed course by slanting to the right. The first man down repeated, "Can I help you with something? What do you want?" He moved to cut off my route.

"Fuck you!!" The words blasted from my lungs where they had been stored up and building pressure for eight weeks. I took off like a startled hare.

Three or four of the workers jumped from the dock and chased me. The man on the ground had a good angle but the element of surprise had left him flatfooted for a couple of seconds and that was all I needed to get by. There was no chance for the dock workers to catch me after that considering our respective states of health and they dropped behind in a hurry.

I got around the corner of the bakery, ran down an alley to the street, and zigzagged for a few blocks until I was completely certain that I was not being followed. I stopped in a storefront doorway to catch my breath. The police would be alerted to the bread truck burglar so I got going again, breathing deeply and running with smooth, powerful strides. It was a joy to be in good shape and I covered many blocks in a short time. I soon found myself in a completely different neighborhood, safe from all but the most unlikely sort of lucky capture.

I slowed to a walk and cut through several alleys looking for clothes on a line. The light was beginning to dawn and I wanted to get a different disguise so I would not get stopped by the police who undoubtly had my description. I found what I was looking for and stole a new pair of pants and a shirt, ducked between two garages, and exchanged my clothes for the second time. I tossed the old clothes in a trash can and walked along until I reached a commercial district.

It was light out now so I stopped in a small cafe for breakfast. I had thiry-five dollars in my pocket and I knew that I wasn't going to be loose for very long so I threw frugality to the wind and ordered the most expensive breakfast on the menu.

Five o'clock in the morning. Platoon 211 had been up for thirty minutes already. They had shit, showered, shaved, done a hundred push-ups, sit-ups, jumping jacks, squat thrusts, toe touches, and deep knee bends. They had also discovered that I

85

was missing. I must have looked foolish sitting there with my quarter-inch haircut and mile-wide grin.

My breakfast came and the waitress asked, "Navy or Marines?"

"Marines—just out of boot."

I was slightly jarred when the fat woman acknowledged me with a bored grunt. I hadn't had time to come to the understanding that to everyone except those actually in the service it meant exactly nothing. Whether one was in Vietnam bleeding to death or stationed at the North Pole or in the plushest embassy in the world, it meant nothing to the rest of America. People like the grunting waitress were far too busy with their own lives to be conscious of us. No doubt there were some people who cared but to most we were merely statistics in the newspaper. Martin Luther King was in the middle of disrupting the country's sadistic adventure with the black man but nobody was about to be bothered with America's other nigger, the service man. Oh well, my breakfast was waiting.

I finished my meal, paid the tab, and walked outside to a world that was brand new. The buildings were washed by the early morning sun and the dew sparkled on the grass and bushes. The increased perception that resulted from near perfect health and escape from a hellish existence made it a very beautiful morning indeed.

I got instructions from a service station and headed toward the ocean. It was about a mile and when I got there I picked out a nice, out-of-the-way place and sat down. I prayed. I sang. I recited poetry out loud. I repeated a few lines of Shakespeare that I knew over and over, dramatizing in the sun.

The world did hold beauty and was worthwhile, no matter who, in their demented hatred, tried to convince me otherwise. I fell into a deep, peaceful sleep.

I woke up with a shadow over me and was a little startled when I realized where I was.

"I'm sorry, I didn't mean to frighten you."

I turned around and saw a thirty-five-year-old woman in

white jogging shorts and dark blue sweatshirt. She had a white headband in her black hair. She looked tan and warm and pretty.

"I thought maybe you were hurt," she said.

I felt embarrassed and stupid and told her I was just sleeping.

"Ok." She turned and started jogging off down the beach.

"Wait a minute," I called out, "I am hurt." I just had to talk to her.

The lady stopped. "What's the matter?" she said as she walked back to where I was sitting.

"Well, I'm hurt because I'm sitting here in the sand feeling stupid and embarrassed and I want to talk to you but I don't know what to say and I don't want you to think that I'm a weirdo...and also because I ran away from Marine boot camp last night."

I could see a flicker of laughter in her eyes for a second. "Why did you do that?"

I thought for a second and decided to tell her the truth even if it did sound crazy and hallucinatory. "Because the hardest part was over and part of me was machine and a little part was human and I wanted to save the human part from turning into machine."

She pondered my answer while I waited for her to run or tell me I was nuts. Instead, to my supreme astonishment, she knelt down in the sand and looked at me with mock seriousness. She said "I think you need to get cleaned up and eat a decent meal." She stood. "C'mon, I live right over here." She pointed to a row of houses near the beach.

I got up and we walked the block or so to her house, exchanging names and other introductory information. Her name was Mrs. Rutherford, call me Sally, and she was from a town near Boston called Worcester. She met her husband, Bob Rutherford, in college and he was now a Commander in the Navy. The place I had chosen for my nap was called La Jolla.

She gave me towels and soap and razor and showed me the shower, said "Cheerio," and disappeared.

I came out of the shower and sat in the kitchen eating my

two hamburgers with coffee while Mrs. Rutherford, call me Sally, got cleaned up from her run on the beach. It was already four o'clock in the afternooon.

The colors in the house seemed to almost jump out at me and the many textures and forms were actually confusing until I settled down enough to enjoy them. After two straight months of cement, dirt, steel and asphalt, all painted green or gray, normal house furnishings were like a sensual assault.

Sally came to the kitchen and poured two cups of coffee, then led me into the comfortable Spanish style living room. She sat on the sofa and I took a chair across from her.

For a few minutes we talked about her two children, Brian and Sandra. They were visiting Bob's parents in San Francisco. Bob was on a cruise and would be back next week. I told her about my family in Minnesota and how I hated to disappoint them so I lied in my letters home. She talked a little about Boston and how much she enjoyed the city.

Then, as if it had been necessary to get all that out of the way before we actually talked, she looked at me and said, "Ok, Danny, now, what happened, how did it happen, and what are you going to do about it?"

I started to tell her about my days in high school, how I didn't seem to fit in any place, the usual adolescent difficulties, and how I decided to solve my teenage problems by joining the marines. I talked and she listened, asking questions now and then and prompting me to get it all out.

I explained that I had begun to doubt my own sanity because I saw the marine training as brainwashing to get us to go into the jungle to be killed. I began to doubt my courage and my manhood because it made much more sense to me to live peacefully if at all possible, and that it seemed very odd for us to go way over to the other side of the world to die for our country when our country was on the other side of the world. I wondered if it was crazy to consider that my individuality was in danger. I told her that the most frightening part of the entire process was how sixty or seventy minds were being shattered and re-formed to make one single mind. I wondered if I was crazy because it was actually real to me, I could actually be aware of, the millions of people who had been slaughtered in war and I really didn't see them as one side good and the other side bad, I just saw them as people being browbeaten or propagandized into killing and being killed.

I poured out the torrent of confusion and bitterness and doubt for three hours. At the end of that time my conclusions were no different from when I started. I simply would not give in to the training no matter what. I did feel much better for having let it out, however, and it even started to look kind of funny.

She listened and understood. When I was finished talking she told me a story that her grandfather had told her when she was a young girl. She told about a man who had to bring a load of wood to a house in the middle of a great city. Since he was new to the city everything he saw or heard was confusing and some of the things would lead him down streets away from his destination. It took the man a long time to figure out that his load was not getting any lighter as he reacted to the many things that surrounded him. Eventually, he got the idea that he should ignore everything and just get to his destination so that he could release his burden, because as long as he had the heavy load on his back he wasn't mobile enough to really understand anything anyhow, no matter how good or bad it appeared to be. So the man blocked out all thought of right or wrong and made his way directly to the house and dropped off his burden. Then, and only then, was he free to really see what was going on around him. As it turned out, getting rid of the heavy bundle was what he actually wanted all the time that he was wandering around looking at other things. "So the point of the whole thing," she said, "is to just keep to yourself and finish boot camp, get rid of the burden, and then, from a distance, you can get it all straight in your mind." Simple.

I knew it was far easier said than done but I also knew she was right. My mind was clearer than it had been in two months.

I felt that I could handle the rest of basic training and told her that I would be going back.

89

Looking across at that beautiful, compassionate woman in the fading sunlight I was deeply moved. That a stranger would show that much simple human kindness to a scrubby looking kid on a beach left me feeling both humble and refreshed. I would do the same for someone some day.

She stood up, walked over and quietly took my hand. We walked down the hallway to her bedroom, an air of peace and innocence surrounding us. She put her arms around my neck and kissed both of my eyes, then placed her open mouth on mine, her tongue hot with ripe womanhood, and we were enveloped in a mushroom cloud of desire. She pulled herself from me and we slowly removed our clothes, baring ourselves in body and in soul. I was on fire with sexual desire but my mind was calm and filled with admiration and caring for her. She told me that as of that moment she saw me as a perfect being, and then she guided our bodies together in the warmth that is unmatched by any other human activity. We moved together in the harmony of the ages and reached an explosive climax of loving pleasure. I lay back and wave after wave of color washed over me, peace replaced turmoil and hate was transformed into love.

With her hand gently rubbing my chest Sally Rutherford whispered in the darkness, "Now you'll be all right."

From some well deep within my soul it started. The dammed up loneliness, sorrow and self-pity that I had suppressed all my life rumbled to the surface. A long, wracking sob tore from my chest and I heaved and shook and cried the tears that I had never dared let out. After several minutes it subsided. I took a breath, blew my nose, felt a giggle come on. Then another and another. We both roared with laughter until our sides hurt.

We got up, got washed and dressed, and had a cup of fresh coffee. I felt ten years old and ten thousand years old. I was flying.

When we were ready we walked out to Sally's car and climbed in. We laughed and talked and sang along with the radio on the way back to the recruit depot. Sooner than either of us wished we were at the front gate.

"Sally, I'll never forget what you've done for me. For sure you saved my sanity and maybe even my life. You're the sweetest, most wonderful person I've ever met." She smiled, almost sadly, and put her fingers to my lips to quiet me.

"Take care of yourself," she said.

"I'm gonna write a book about you someday," I joked.

She laughed. "Goodbye."

"Goodbye, Sally."

I got out of the car, hitched up my stolen pants, and strolled over to the MP at the gate. "My name's Private O'Brian and I'm AWOL."

CHAPTER TEN

...the Knave was standing before them, in chains, with a soldier on each side to guard him; and near the King was the White Rabbit, with a trumpet in one hand, and a scroll of parchment in the other.

I was held in what was called the bullpen overnight. There were ten other misguided young marines in there who were being held for such things as theft, assault, and a host of other offenses that only a marine could commit, such as being late for muster, not returning from a weekend in town, talking back to an officer and so on.

We talked for some time about our criminal activites. I was the only recruit hence I was given a ton of advice on how to survive the ordeal intact. It was enjoyable talking to the other prisoners but I didn't think their advice could be very valid since they had gotten themselves locked up every bit as tight as I had, some for even dumber things than running away in the middle of the night. There was a common agreement that the Marine Corps presented one with a fairly obnoxious life style and the sooner that part of one's life was a thing of the past the better. Eventually the circle of talkers dwindled down and I moved away to get some sleep and figure out how I could get back in the good graces of my DIs without doing a stretch on the rock pile.

In the morning I awoke to the cry of "2110295." That was me. I stood near the cage door and was confronted by a stout, ugly PFC who said menacingly, "Ok prisoner, come with me." He led me down a dank, green corridor to an office. He opened the door and pushed me inside. I was greeted by none other than Sgt. Liebermann, who stared icily at me.

"Don't you like your platoon, O'Brian?"

"Sir, I like it fine."

"Then why did you go over the hill?"

I put on my most groveling look. "Sir, my girl back home is pregnant and I had to call to see if she was going to be all right, sir."

"Don't lie to me, cocksucker, why didn't you call her from here if you were so fucking worried?"

"Sir, I didn't think I could."

"You're lying, maggot!"

"Yes, sir. I was afraid to ask the drill instructor sir, because I was afraid the drill instructor would think my mind was elsewhere, sir."

"Your mind was elsewhere wasn't it shitbird?"

"Yes, sir."

"How come it took you damn near twenty-four hours to call home, boy?"

"Sir, I was afraid to come back."

WHAM! Liebermann hit me solidly in the left cheekbone with his fist and knocked me like a shot to the floor. I was unconscious for at least a ten count. I hadn't even seen his fist coming until it was a split second from exploding in my face. I gradually came to consciousness with him yelling at me.

"How come you're taking a nap, turd? You must be tired from playing yesterday, is that it?"

"No, sir."

"Then get up, snake!"

I climbed to my feet and tried to stand at attention. I was afraid now because I knew I had gone a long way beyond what the DIs would excuse. I had no idea whether he was going to continue to beat on me or what.

"You deserted your platoon you fucking rattlesnake, therefore you can no longer be trusted. If we were in a state of declared war I could have you taken outside and shot by a firing squad.

As it is I'm gonna have you court-martialed and I'm gonna recommend a sentence of not less than seven years in Leavenworth Federal Penitentiary and a dishonorable discharge."

He was serious! This was way beyond my wildest imagination. I started to cry and begged him.

"No...please, sir. I won't ever do it again. Please don't destroy my life!"

"You brought it on yourself, kid. You want to dance the jig in the Marine Corps you're gonna have to pay the fuckin' fiddler. If I thought you were worth saving I'd ask for a lighter sentence but you don't show me shit."

I dropped the crybaby routine and looked him straight in the eye. "Sir, if you give me a break I'll be the best marine in the corps. I love the Marines, sir, and I don't want to get kicked out."

Apparently he believed me. "We'll see, asshole," he said, and walked out of the room.

I was left at a position of attention and I didn't dare move for fear that I was being watched somehow. The more I thought about it the more ridiculous it got. I was AWOL for less than twenty-four hours and that idiot had me intimidated into thinking about seven years in prison. A short stretch on the local rock-breaking gang was not inconceivable, which would be bad enough, but seven years in prison was too much for a raw recruit to believe. The return of my senses was welcome.

The ugly PFC came into the room swinging his billy club. I had an urge to let him have a left hook right in the middle of his pimples but thought better of the idea.

"Get your hands behind your back, puke," he said gruffly. I put my hands back and he snapped on a pair of handcuffs with a flourish that he had seen somebody else originate. He poked me in the back with the stick. "March, motherfucker."

He directed me across the base to a quonset hut near 211's platoon street, poking me now and then and growling. When we got there he unlocked the cuffs and told me to stand at attention while he moved off several feet to one side, ready to spring into action if I tried to run away.

Staff Sgt. Radrich, who was kind of an administrative boss for our series of platoons, poked his head out the door of the hut and said, "We're ready."

The guard shoved me toward the door and I walked over and stepped inside. Sgt. Radrich said, "Report to the Commanding Officer," indicating with a nod which door I was supposed to go in. I walked in, centered myself in front of the desk, and shouted, "Sir, Private O'Brian reporting as ordered."

The CO was Lieutenant Handall, the weak-looking little man who had inspected our rifles at the three week point in training.

"Private O'Brian," the Lt. said solemnly, "I understand that you were on an unauthorized absence yesterday. I also understand that you have some kind of a problem with a pregnant girl friend. I want you to explain what's going on here."

I told the Lieutenant about how the worry about my girl friend back home in Minneapolis had just about driven me crazy and how finally it started to affect my performance as a recruit. When it reached the point where I could no longer concentrate during the classes I decided I had to get away so I could call and find out what was happening. The letters I had received weren't really explaining anything so a phone call was the only way out.

"Why the hell didn't you speak up if you had a problem?"

"Sir, I was afraid the drill instructor would think I was just trying to skate out, sir."

"Where did you get those clothes?"

"Sir, I bought them from a guy on the street."

"Well, since you came back on your own and you were gone for less than twenty-four hours I'm going to fine you fifty dollars and send you back to your platoon. If there is ever a next time you'll be doing some time in the brig. Dismissed."

"Thank you, sir."

"I said dismissed, you weird fuck."

"Aye, aye, sir." I turned and walked out the door, my heart soaring. I wouldn't even have to break rocks.

When I reported back to platoon street it was empty so I quickly took out a clean pair of utilities and put them on. They felt much better than jailhouse clothes ever would. I ran up to the dumpster behind the head and threw away my third set of clothes in twenty-four hours. I knew I was bound for an ass-kicking but nonetheless I still felt good.

In a short while the platoon returned from a class and I walked out and took my place in the formation with a deadpan expression.

I was back in the groove. Back on the main street, moving toward the end of the line where I would dump my burden and be done with it. It was a big relief to know I was off the hook, but at the same time I knew that the next weeks were going to be rough. I would have to be constantly vigilant to protect the secret of my lack of acceptance of the training from the DIs. What was equally important was keeping the other members of the platoon from seeing that I was rejecting the idea of being a military machine. If it was discovered that I was calling bullshit on the whole scene, lock, stock, and barrel, I would be assigned to the fat farm so fast it would spin my head.

CHAPTER ELEVEN

"It's—it's a very fine day!" said a timid voice at her side. She was walking by the White Rabbit, who was peeping anxiously into her face.

"Very," said Alice. "Where's the Duchess?"

"Hush! Hush!" said the Rabbit in a low, hurried tone. He looked anxiously over his shoulder as he spoke, and then raised himself upon tiptoe, put his mouth close to her ear, and whispered, "She's under sentence of execution."

Private Philip Bradfern was slower and less bright than most of the recruits in 211 and as a result he was singled out for harassment more than usual. He had managed to stay with the platoon because of his excellent attitude and willing spirit. He avoided trouble by giving his all in every endeavor and by keeping his mouth shut and his eyes and ears open. He learned and succeeded because of sheer tenacity.

However, as the demands of training became steeper I noticed a flicker of resentment cross his face from time to time which he quickly hid from the instructors. As time wore on the resentment seemed to come more often and last longer and get hidden less well. I was certain that the drill instructors had noticed, and figured it would only be a matter of time before a crisis point was reached with the private.

One day Sgt. Barton ordered us to fall out on platoon street with our backpacks, sweatshirts, and tennis shoes. We were going for a run. Bradfern was angry. He openly complained about how horseshit it was to have to run in the heat when no other platoons were doing it. Since we were supposed to maintain silence while getting our gear together the DI must have heard him carping about the unfairness of the situation.

We started to march and when we reached the open road Sgt. Barton gave the command to double-time. We ran for about half a mile until we were halted near a sandpit.

We loaded sand in our backpacks and the DI checked them to make sure that everyone had the sand packed down hard and right to the top. The packs held about twenty-five pounds of the same so with that dead weight strapped to our backs it was difficult to run.

We had gone perhaps five miles when Bradfern dropped out of formation and lay on the ground panting and sweating. Sgt. Barton halted the platoon and ran back to Private Bradfern to see if he was hurt. When the DI was sure that the private was not physically injured he told him to get up on his feet and join the rest of the platoon. Bradfern struggled to his feet and immediately collapsed again. The DI once again told him to get on his feet. For the first time Bradfern lost control of himself.

"I can't, sir." he cried.

"Get on your fuckin' feet magpie or I'll tear your goddam head off and feed it to the rats!"

Bradfern, laid out flat on his back, screamed in the DI's face, "I can't take this fuckin' shit anymore! Leave me alone!"

Sgt. Barton reached down and grabbed Bradfern by the collar of his sweatshirt and dragged the private back to the platoon. He threw him into the rank where he belonged.

Bradfern fell to the ground immediately, defiant and apparently set on calling the DI's bluff. Sgt. Barton started us running again and several privates ran right over Bradfern, who stayed on the ground. Sgt. Barton stayed behind with him and we continued back to platoon street, led by our right guide. We dumped the sand near our area and ran home. We changed back into our normal uniforms and waited for the DI to return.

Sgt. Barton and Bradfern came along shortly. The DI was

100

cursing and kicking the recruit in the ass and Bradfern was stumbling along with tears turning his dirty face to mud.

We were sent to the shower to clean up and prepare for chow. Private Bradfern was sent on his own after we had finished.

As we got ready to march over to the mess hall Sgt. Barton said, "Phil, you walk with me." Bradfern fell out of formation and went over to the DI.

"Aye, aye, sir." Bradfern said tentatively.

"You don't have to sir me, Phil. You don't want to be a turd anyway since you're too good to run with them. You just call me John, Phil."

"Aye, aye...s...John."

We marched to the chow hall with Sgt. Barton and Private Bradfern walking alongside. When we arrived the DI sent us in and took Bradfern with him to eat in the drill instructors' private dining room. After dinner Bradfern walked back to the platoon area with the DI.

For the next two days Bradfern was allowed to smoke at will and had at least a full pack each day urged on him by the DIs. He never joined the platoon in physical exercise or classes, he ate in the DIs' mess, drank coffee while we cleaned the area up, and in general was treated with the utmost courtesy.

By the third day Private Bradfern's nerves had been stretched to the breaking point. He had a hunted look in his eyes. I assume that he would gladly have traded places with some unfortunate victim on the rack if it had been in his power to choose the mode of skewering that he surely was going to get.

Sgt. Barton was back on duty the third day and right after breakfast he found an excuse to punish us. He sent us over to the sandpits and divided the platoon into two even groups, putting one in each pit. He made us do push-ups and had Private Bradfern count for us while he disappeared. Each time Bradfern opened his mouth to count he dug a deeper hole for himself. Platoon 211 was adding up everything the recruit did or didn't do that we couldn't or had to do.

The DI returned to the pits with two frosty glasses of lemonade and two director's chairs. He and Bradfern sat in the canvas chairs sipping lemonade and puffing on cigarettes.

"Why don't we have them thrash, Phil?"

"Aye, aye, John."

"You go ahead and tell them, Phil."

"Thrash!"

We thrashed until the dust and sand choked us and filled our clothes.

"Tell the turds to thrash harder, Phil."

"Thrash harder, turds!"

211 flopped around in the sand. We were nearing insanity.

"Phil, will you please tell the maggots to stop thrashing and get on their feet?"

"Stop and get up on your feet, maggots!"

We stood panting and in pain while Bradfern watched, hands on hips. Sgt. Barton moved the chairs and glasses back about ten feet behind the private, then surveyed us.

The DI pointed and said quietly, "You may have Private Bradfern."

The next thing I knew there was a massive pileup of bodies all kicking and squirming and punching. Private Bradfern was on the bottom.

Sgt. Barton called us to attention and we all unpiled with the bloody exception of Phil, who was, unfortunately, very unconscious.

"Oh my, oh my, oh my, Private Bradfern must have run into a door. A couple of you pukes scrape him up and take him to sick bay."

Bradfern started to wake up and the two designated recruits helped the dazed and sorry turd to the infirmary.

Private Bradfern did not return to 211 and we never did hear another word about him.

❂   ❂   ❂

April, 1966

The "dirty little war" slowly and certainly escalated after

the monsoon rains passed and the sun took over as our chief natural misery.

The end of the driving, blinding sheets of rain seemed to mark the termination of our enthusiasm for life in the bush. The company's casualty list began to mount and as we were picked off, one ·by one, we gradually became aware that the grinning skull of death waited for us nearly every time we crossed the barbed concertina wire that surrounded the base camp. Allenson, Baker, Connelly, Diaz... we threw their gear in seabags, tagged them with "name, KIA, patrol, vicinity Chu Lai," and sent the bags to headquarters.

C company—"Suicide Charlie"—the pride of Guadalcanal, the asskickers of the Chosin Reservoir, was slowly but surely disintegrating. As each new casualty was brought in something in our minds grew tighter and more violent. The only way to release the tremendous amount of malevolent energy that was built up in our collective psyche was to burn, shoot, blow up, slash, and destroy the enemy every time he gave us even the slightest opportunity.

Lance Corporal Moren, a tall, quiet nineteen-year-old from Texas was unable to shake off the death of his best friend, Pete Haller. They had enlisted in the Corps together on the "buddy system" and had been in the same units since the first day of basic training.

At the end of a long, uneventful patrol Haller's squad was winding its way along a well-worn path in a grassy area about fifty yards east of the perimeter. It was about three o'clock in the afternoon and waves of heat could be seen shimmering like a mirage in the distance. The only thing moving in the blistering, needle-like sunrays was the marine patrol. And one other man, or woman, or child. The sniper sighted in, fired, and hit Pete Haller in the back of the neck, killing him instantly. There was no pain. There was not even a possibility that Pete knew what happened to him. He simply went from living to dead faster than can be comprehended. The smashing of Haller's neckbone caused the bullet to break into fragments and lodge in the large muscles of the neck and upper back. The only wound was a hole about the size of a pencil. Otherwise he was unmarked. Until the bruises came he looked to be sleeping peacefully.

The patrol poured hundreds of rounds of return fire into the tree line where the sniper had apparently been but no sign of the silent assassin was ever found.

It was not at all unusual for those of us who lost friends in Vietnam to weep openly and without shame. We had seen too much to still subscribe to the TV images of manliness that we grew up with, and we hadn't seen enough, yet, to grow completely insensitive. That particular form of moral and spiritual death did not catch up with us until later. It was unusual, though, for someone to be unable to shut off the flow of grief after a few days. Moren was absolutely crushed by the death of his friend. I think that if Haller had died shattered and bloody it would have been more acceptable to Bill. For some odd and inexplicable reason the physical simplicity of the way he died made the finality of his death unreal to his partner.

Unlike "normal" people we did not start whispering and worrying when Moren's depression refused to lift. We respected his right to handle the loss in any way that he saw fit.

It seemed like a good sign when Bill's state of mind turned to a kind of intense bitterness that he directed at the VC and NVA soldiers. He volunteered for every patrol. He took extra watches on the odd chance that Charlie would probe us. He became the kind of marine that the recruit training camps love to produce.

It was obvious to us, when we had the benefit of hindsight, that Bill was getting too intense for his own good. He lost weight, lost his sense of humor, didn't sleep enough, and was pushing much too hard. Before he cracked, though, it just seemed like a good thing that he was getting over Haller's sniping.

One night we caught a company-sized patrol of North Vietnamese soldiers in an ambush. We had been after them for a long time and our reconnaissance units finally paid off in spades by gathering information we needed to catch the entire enemy group together. Alpha and Charlie Companies were set up in a well-planned position along a ridge line that ran parallel to a swiftly flowing river. Once the NVA company passed a cemetary at the south end of our trap a platoon from Alpha moved into position and sealed off any hope of escape through the back way Fifty caliber machine guns were placed at the north end to provide enfilade fire and close off that route. The river on the east, and over two hundred marines on the western ridge, slammed the coffin door.

When the NVA showed up it was like a dream come true for us. The incredible tension that had built up for weeks was released in an orgy of violence. The controlled, disciplined fire that was supposed to take place never did. We were trained to deliver the first volley at waist level, then aim in at ground level on the second volley. Very neat and very effective.

The first round was fired by our CO as a signal for the rest of us to open up. Usually the firing would build up for about five seconds, hold steady for a few seconds more, die down, build up on the second volley, then peter out if we weren't taking incoming rounds. A cease fire would then cut the firing off completely and after a short wait we would go count bodies. This time the first volley started out fine but something went wrong. A mass hysteria gripped us and seemed to shake every last inhibition from our brains. The sound of gunfire built up and up until we were engulfed in one ear-splitting, mind-shattering explosion of sound. All discipline and caution were thrown to the winds. People were standing up, firing from the hip, screaming, shrieking with the blood lust of the murderously insane. We slapped in magazines of twenty rounds and pumped them into the fire zone as fast as our fingers could pull the triggers. The shouting of the officers to cease fire was drowned out in the roar. On and on it went until our ammunition and bitterness was spent. When the madness was finally brought under control we sank down onto the thick soft floor of the jungle and caught our breath.

I heard a giggle. Then another. I laughed softly with relief. It wasn't really funny to slaughter a hundred and fifty people. It was just an eerie, scary relief.

The mop-up operation took the rest of the night. We had

105

to fish some of the NVA out of the river, pick up arms and legs, and get an accurate count. There were 132 dead NVA. No wounded, no prisoners. The weak return fire had wounded six marines.

We got back to the base camp well after dawn and were cleaning our weapons when we got the word—Bill Moren was medevaced. Captain Johnson, who had been CO for the last couple of months, had personally escorted LCpl Moren to the field hospital back by the chopper base. We knew Bill wasn't one of the men who were hit during the ambush so we took it for granted he had had an appendicitis attack or something. We had breakfast and hit the rack, dismissing Moren for the time being.

I was brought from a deep sleep by someone shouting, "Hey, let's go you guys, we got a muster right away. C'mon, move it." We had only slept about three hours. "What the fuck, a goddam muster now?" Smitty mumbled, still foggy with sleep.

We assembled on a road near Capt. Johnson's hootch and waited for something to happen. It was highly unusual to get harassed in Vietnam by military bullshit so we knew something unusual was in the wind.

The CO came out. "Listen up," he said, "The shit's hitting the fan down at Battalion right now so pay attention. The Colonel got the word on what happened last night. He wants you to know that the operation was highly successful and that it was the best kill in a long time. He also wants you to know that any further breakdown in fire discipline will result in somebody's ass being had. The ass that's had isn't gonna be mine so I'm telling you right now, from fire team leaders to platoon commanders, that you'd better settle down."

He pawed at the ground with his boot. "We had a man break down last night. LCpl Moren was medevaced to the psych ward. He was caught mutilating KIAs. The only reason I don't have him up on charges right now is because his platoon commander talked me out of it, and I believed his story. But," he shook his finger at us, "if it ever happens again, as long as I'm com-

106

manding this unit, you're gonna be court-martialed and sent to the brig. That's all I've got. Go back to sleep.''

We were dismissed by the company gunney and headed back to our hootches.

I saw a small knot of marines talking to the 1st Sgt. and walked over to them. I caught Bob Gunderson who was close to Moren and Haller, as he broke away from the group.

"Hey, Bob," I asked him, "they talking about Moren?"

"Yeah," he replied, a confused expression in his eyes.

"He was cuttin' a gook?"

Gunderson nodded.

"What'd he do to him?"

Gunderson stopped, shook his head, looked down at the ground, and said in a choked voice, "He chopped his fuckin' head off!"

CHAPTER TWELVE

"Dear, dear! How queer everything is today! And yesterday things went on just as usual. I wonder if I've changed in the night? Let me think: was I the same when I got up this morning? I almost think I can remember feeling a little different. But if I'm not the same, the next question is, 'Who in the world am I?'...."

Every time that I wrote home I felt more guilty because I was lying about how much I enjoyed boot camp and each letter was a cover-up of the letters that preceded it. What had started out as concern for the peace of mind of my family grew into an outlandish false portrayal of my role. In order to preserve the image I had built in their minds I found myself getting deeper and deeper into the fantasy.

Dear Mom and Dad,
Well, I got a little free time here and I thought I'd drop you a line to let you know that everything is still ok. I got your last letter. Thanks. I went over the hill last week. AWOL. Don't be upset because it's not as bad as it sounds. I just went over the fence for a couple of hours on a dare. I sure did catch hell when I got back. It wasn't a very smart thing to do but I've heard that every good marine does it sometime and I just happened to get it out of my system

early. I got fined fifty bucks by my commanding officer and that taught me a lesson. It won't goof me up as far as going up the ranks is concerned at least and I'm glad because I've got my eye on those Sergeant's stripes.

Our platoon is getting more squared away all the time and it looks as though we have a good chance to take honor platoon if we win final drill. We've washed out all the screwups by now so it's just a matter of polishing our techniques.

It sure is hard on the rest of the group when there's a few people around who can't hack the training. I'm really glad that we dumped them all. You just can't go into combat without discipline. If you've got a handful of guys who think they can do their own thing the whole unit is gonna get shot to hell.

This isn't the most pleasant thing in the world to do and it would be stupid to think that it is but I'm willing to make a sacrifice for my country. I've heard about some of the radicals in the dink factories (colleges) who are going around saying that the service is bad and degrading and all that. I think they should try it first before they shoot off their mouths. I don't feel degraded by our training at all, as a matter of fact I feel proud that I can be a marine. As far as us being killers, well, it's a fact that we are trained to kill. That's our job. The gooks are trained to kill also and that's their job. There isn't any reason to get sentimental about the whole thing. What those college punks don't realize is that we have a Commander in Chief named Lyndon Johnson who knows one heck of a lot more about what's going on in the world than they do. We have intelligence agencies that give information on Vietnam and so forth to the President that the know-it-all college set *isn't aware of. I suppose the next thing you know those people are going to start questioning the intelligence network and FBI and everyone else. I wish they'd just study their algebra and leave the world problems to the President and the killing to us. Whew. That was quite a speech. I get kind of wound up now and then.*

Well, I suppose it's starting to thaw out up north now so you should be enjoying the weather soon. Say hello to everyone.

Love,
Danny

On Sunday afternoon we were out on the street polishing our gear when the word came from the duty hut that I was wanted by the platoon commander.

I wondered if they had found some way to read my mind and wanted to have a chat with me about what I had been thinking. What I'd been debating with myself about was how I had managed to get myself tangled up in such an asshole situation while millions of people the same age were still in high school driving their hot rods around, drinking beer on Saturday nights, and taking nice looking chicks to the drive-in movies and making out. I was thinking about what a bunch of hateful, spiteful, chickenshit people were running the miserable insane asylum I was stuck in. I took it one step further and fantasized about loading my M-14 and putting a 7.62 millimeter slug right in Sgt. Barton's forgiving father brain and then chopping Sgt. Liebermann into bloody little pieces of meat and gristle with a poleax.

I pulled myself out of the violent little dream and ran to the duty hut. I knocked three times. "Sir, Private O'Brian reporting as ordered."

"You got a visitor, asshole. Follow the yellow line around

the grinder and it'll take you to the visiting area. Lay off the pogey bait. If I see you with a snickers or something like that I'll kick your skinny little ass up to your ears. Now get the fuck outa here."

"Aye, aye, sir." I couldn't imagine who would be visiting me here since I didn't have any relatives or friends that I knew of in California.

I took off for the visiting area at double-time, happy for a break in the monotony. Talking to someone besides my fellow turds, even for an hour, might be very pleasant.

I got to the spot set aside for visitors, checked in with the corporal in charge, and started looking around for a familiar face.

"Hi, Danny."

It was Tom Wilbertson, a high school friend who had joined the Navy six months or so before I went into the service. He looked about the same as always except that his head was clipped in the familiar "white sidewall" cut, and he was wearing the blue bell-bottomed pants and flap shirt of the Navy. He still had his crooked grin that seemed to indicate he had gotten away with something.

I was happy to see him and we had a pleasant talk about the old days and how things were in Minneapolis while he was on leave. He told me about the girls he fucked back home and how he was looking forward to going overseas to Hong Kong and other exotic ports of call to fuck a lot more girls. We laughed and smoked and had a thoroughly good time.

The conversation eventually got around to comparing our respective branches of service and we both started lying. Tom told me how great it was to work aboard a giant aircraft carrier, to travel the world and find adventure on the high seas. It was also vital to the defense to have aircraft within striking distance of an enemy area when there was no land base for the jet fighters. He explained how hundreds of gooks could be wiped out with a single bomb.

I told him of the terrific future in store for me as one of the world's greatest fighting men. Almost two hundred years had proved that no matter how great the barrage of artillery or air-craft or ship fire, there was, in the final analysis, only one way to defeat the enemy. That was where the role of the marine rifleman came in. In order to close with and destroy the enemy he had to be dug out of his holes and bunkers and shot or sprayed with a flamethrower or killed in some other intimate, personal way. I told how the marines were first to fight and were always the President's number one choice when it came time for the dirty, close in fighting that separated the men from the boys.

When the alloted time was up we shook hands and went our separate ways, Tom back to his life as an exotic young stud that sailed the ocean blue, and me to my machismo adventure as a killer marine.

On my way out of the compound I had a strong impulse to turn around and run back to Wilbertson and tell him that I was lying and that I knew he was too. Instead, I shrugged my shoul-ders and started running for platoon street, steeling myself for the push-ups and chewing out that I knew was in store for me as a result of having a visitor while the rest of the platoon didn't.

CHAPTER THIRTEEN

*"I can't explain myself, I'm afraid, Sir," said Alice, because
I'm not myself, you see."*

"I don't see," said the Caterpillar.

*"I'm afraid I can't put it more clearly," Alice replied very
politely, "for I can't understand it myself to begin with; and
being so many different sizes in a day is very confusing."*

"It isn't," said the Caterpillar.

*"Well, perhaps you haven't found it so yet," said Alice: "but
when you have to turn into a chrysalis—you will some day,
you know—and then after that into a butterfly, I should think
you'll feel it a little queer, won't you?"*

"Ready...seats!"

We folded to a sitting position, sixty butts hitting the floor
at precisely the same instant. We had practiced sitting down so
many hundreds of times at mealtimes, classes, and shit calls that
it had become second nature for the entire platoon to act as one
person.

"At ease."

SLAP! Our open hands clapped our thighs in one so that
it sounded like a giant slap.

We were at a class to learn the manly art of destroying the
enemy with our bare hands. This ability was to be taught by
Sgt. Fox, whom we had heard of through the recruit grapevine.

The instructor came bounding into the specially equipped

former mess hall wearing a karate uniform with a black belt. He sported a cleanly shaven, tanned head and a giant black handle, bar moustache. He was grinning widely.

"Good morning, recruits!"

"Good morning, sir."

He exuded confidence and enthusiasm as he paced the floor at the head of the class with effortless energy.

"Now the first thing I'm going to ask you to do is to remove your boots and socks, unbutton the top button of your utility jackets, remove your belts, and take the tails of your jackets out of your trousers. Place your gear in the rear of the room in your platoon order, and return to the position that you now occupy. I would like you to do this now."

When we had completed that preliminary task and returned to the mats on which we had been sitting Sgt. Fox began his class.

"Privates, I'm going to ask you to do something which you haven't done much of in the past weeks of your basic training. I'm going to ask you to use your minds." He smiled and we howled. "I realize that you may be a little rusty but try anyhow. Imagine yourself in a foxhole at three o'clock in the morning. You can't see a damned thing and yet you know that those gooks out there have no love in their hearts for you. Let's face it, we're all about the same, and all of us, every swinging dick in this room, is going to have one thing in common in a situation like that. Every one of us is gonna be a little nervous, if not out and out scared shitless. So there you are, in a foxhole, scared, maybe cold and hungry...and definitely horny as a two-peckered billy goat. You're daydreaming about that little gal back home and wishing you were there—when all of a sudden all hell breaks loose; bullets flying everywhere, people yelling, some getting hit and screaming with pain, mortars and artillery going off, and your unit is badly outnumbered. The enemy makes a human wave assualt and eventually you get overrun. You suddenly find that, like it or not, you've got a gook face to face with you that had malice in his black little heart. Just what do you suppose you're gonna do?" He paused to let it sink in. "Two days ago that exact thing happened twenty miles south of

116

Danang. We lost fourteen men but we would have lost a hell of a lot more if they had not paid attention in this class."

He motioned Private Lagerquist to the front and arranged it so that the recruit's hands were around his neck.

The instructor continued, "What are you gonna do if a gook had you like this, right by the throat, and is fixin' to choke the life out of you?" Faster than the eye could follow he broke the private's grip, threw him to the floor, and roared, "KILL THE DIRTY LITTLE BASTARD!" Three swift motions with his right hand and Private Lagerquist was, for all intents and purposes, dead as a stone.

Sgt. Fox helped the private to his feet with a twinkly little smile and sent him, shaken but unhurt, back to his position.

"Now don't ever get the idea, don't even let it cross your mind, that anything less than complete destruction of the enemy is adequate. Once you get him down make sure that he stays down. There's more than one marine burning in hell right now for making the mistake of stopping before the enemy was completely dead. Do you follow me?"

"Yes, sir." We not only followed, we were fascinated by the colorful instructor.

"When we get finished with this series of classes you will have the tools that are necessary for your survival in hand-to-hand combat. I cannot stress enough that the main thing that will determine whether you live or die in this type of situation is your desire to kill the enemy. This is of the utmost importance and is of greater value to you than all the technical skills in the world would be without the killer instinct. If I can only get it through your heads that the only time you will be safe is when your opponent is no longer breathing and his heart is stopped, if I can get you to realize that much, then you will be sufficiently enlightened to do your jobs as marines."

Sgt. Fox gave his instructions like a football coach talking about the big game. He was so bright, energetic, and strikingly happy that it was impossible not to be swept along in the tide of his enthusiasm. He liked what he was doing enormously and so we liked it too.

117

He got Private Keller up front for the next demonstration. "Pay very close attention now privates. Every technique you will learn ends with the three basic steps that I'm going to show you now." He whipped Keller to the mat. "When you get the enemy to the deck always maintain bodily contact with him, like so." He twisted Keller's arm and held it in an iron grip so that he couldn't squirm away. "With your free hand," he waved, "you go...EEYAH! EEYAH! EEYAH!" His screams pierced the room. In three vicious rips he had disemboweled, and thus murdered, the enemy.

"More slowly now," he said. "You maintain bodily contact all the way down, don't let him get away from you...with the free hand you, one...tear the groin area and genitals...two, smash with extended fingers into the soft area just below the breastbone known as the solar plexus...and three, claw the throat area, digging in on both sides of the Adam's apple and tearing apart the larynx. Did you see that?"

"Yes sir," we answered.

"If you position yourself properly, apply the blows with the correct leverage and hand formation, and, above all, do not show even the slightest hint of mercy, the three body areas will yield and you will have a dead gook. Remember, these three thrusts are the basis of all hand-to-hand combat, Marine Corps style. Don't worry if it was too fast for you because you will practice all of the techniques we've shown and many more so much that you'll be doing them in your sleep."

We were split up into two pairs and learned some of the fundamentals of fighting at close range. We practiced falls, escapes, methods of sparring, and various throws. We practiced, over and over again, the final three moves. Groin, solar plexus, throat.

In the following days we learned many more techniques that were designed to confuse and hurt an opponent and we practiced until the gentle art of hand killing became second nature. At the end of the last class Sgt. Fox again addressed us. He thanked us for our courteous attention, wished us well, and told us that he would be seeing us in future classes.

The martial arts classes had a profound effect on the platoon. After thousands of repetitions we had the moves down cold but, even more significant, we had developed the killer instinct. We had gained the calm and confidence that came with the certainty that we were dangerous. Knowing that we could kill a man with no weapon other than our bare hands gave us a quality that we had not had previously. We gained a kind of perverse mastery over life itself that reflected in our everyday demeanor and allowed us to indulge in the fantasy that we were, indeed, larger than life. After all, that was what being a marine was all about.

We arrived at the mess hall shortly after leaving the hand-to-hand combat class and, since we were early, the DI had us stand outside and read our little red books. The small books had information in them such as drill maneuvers, Marine Corps history, explanations of the tools and weapons we would use, chain of command and so on. We were required to have the red book on our person at all times and we had it pretty well memorized toward the end of training.

Private McCormick, who had been kicked in the stomach accidentally, suddenly without warning, threw up. He sprayed a thin, smelly mixture of bile and sour food on the sidewalk and as soon as he was finished he wiped his chin and continued reading. The violent incident took only a few seconds.

Sgt. Barton walked briskly over to McCormick, his face flushed with annoyance. "How come you splashed your smelly puke on my sidewalk, animal?"

"Sir, I was sick."

"I hate turds that got no respect for my sidewalk. Get your ass over to that squad bay and get a bucket and swab to pick that shit up. Nobody wants your drippin's spoiling their lunch!"

McCormick ran to the nearest squad bay and came back with a bucket of water and a mop to clean up his mess. The smell was terrible.

Sgt. Barton gave us a speech on hygiene and how he was going to kick ass on anyone that puked on his property in the future. Sidewalks were for walking on, toilets were for puking into. He ordered us into the mess hall for lunch.

119

We got done eating and were waiting for the DI to come out from the instructor's mess and tell us what to do. We were reading our books again.

Just as Sgt. Barton rounded the corner of the chow hall Private McCormick threw up again. This time there was only a small amount of the evil substance and it amounted to not more than the half cup of soup McCormick had eaten for lunch. The frightened private, who had apparently taken the DI's speech to heart, caught the vomit in his cupped hands. Before Sgt. Barton had a chance to say anything McCormick jammed both his hands in his pockets, spilling only a tiny amount of puke on the ground. McCormick wiped his hands on his pant legs and the DI chose to ignore it.

Sgt. Barton gave us a right face with a small smile on his face and started us down the road. When we passed the sick bay he halted the platoon and sent Private McCormick in to see the corpsman. Without a word he started us up again and we headed for the next class.

It was raining, so we were inside the quonset huts polishing our gear when Sgt. Barton called for us to come out to platoon street. He marched us to a classroom and took his standard position in front of the room.

"Girls," he intoned, "all of the tests that you took in the first week of your vacation here in sunny California have been evaluated. You have been assigned MOSes based on your performance in the tests. MOS stands for Military Occupation Specialty and designates the type of job that you'll be doing while you're in the Marine Corps. For right now you'll be given a four-number code and until you are actually assigned to a unit or finish school the last two numbers of the code will be zeros. Listen up while the names and MOSes are called 'cause I'm only going to do it one time."

He read the names off in alphabetical order, telling each private what his job number was. The majority of the platoon had the number 0300. When he got to my name he said it was going to be a 2500.

"Sir, Private Koyner requests to know what 0300 is."

"Grunt."

"Sir?"

"Grunt, stupid. Infantry. It means you put a pack on your back and walk up and down hills grunting. It also means you're gonna walk your young ass into the bush to seek out, close with, and destroy the enemy. Any of you people with 0300 MOSes had best keep alert when you're being instructed cause you're settin' sail for gooksville sooner or later. Some of you will be trained as riflemen, some as machine gunners, some as grenade launchers or mortarmen, all of you for sure are going to be in an infantry company.

"Sir, Private Jackson requests to know what 6700 means."

The DI consulted his clipboard with a puzzled expression on his brow. He looked up, disgust marring his features, and said, "Electronics, asshole. You'll be going to a radar school in Alabama. That's a damn good assignment for a cunt so you'll probably be successful for once in your miserable fuckin' life. You're the only turd in the platoon that's going to a pussy school so take it for what it's worth."

Sgt. Barton fielded questions on job specialties for thirty minutes or so, giving sarcastic answers to the privates who had supply, clerk, or mechanical MOSes. He brought up his own specialty with pride. He was actually a demolitions expert and was assigned to the recruit depot for two years as a reward for his work in setting up mine fields during a special mission to Vietnam as an advisor. He belittled the recruits with what he called the "candy corps" jobs.

Three other turds had the same number as mine and I waited for one of them to ask what it was. Apparently we were of like mind because none of them spoke up and finally I had to.

"2500 is a radioman. You'll either come right back here for school as a teletype operator or you'll go to a unit as a field radio operator which means you strap it on your back and grunt like the rest. You'll know which way you're going in a minute when I give you your duty stations."

121

In one of our recent classes the instructor had talked about casualties in an amphibious landing. During the lecture he pointed out that in theory the one with the shortest life span was the commanding officer. The prize for the second shortest life expectancy was the radioman. I had barely been listening but now it came back to me with a rush.

"These are the two that you want to knock out first, the officer commanding the unit and the communications man. The gooks will be trying to do the same thing. If you can disrupt the leadership and then isolate the unit you stand a good chance of blowing the whole outfit away."

That was not good news at all. For the eight millionth time I wished that I had not joined the Marine Corps.

"If you girls want to stop milling around like a bunch of fuckin' cattle I'll read your duty stations to you." We held still. "After completion of infantry training you will all be given two weeks leave. At the end of your leave you will report to your place of assignment. It's still a long way off but I'll tell you anyhow. Don't be late reporting in to your very first unit. If you go waltzing in to duty station right after boot camp and you're a day or two days or even an hour late you're in for big trouble."

He read the list of duty stations, again in alphabetical order. Most of the turds were going to Camp Pendleton. A few to Camp Lejeune. Two to San Diego MCRD for school. One private had the good fortune to be assigned to San Francisco. One was going to Portsmouth, New Hampshire as a prison guard. Private Ward was going to Alaska. I was going to the desert training facilities at Twentynine Palms, in the middle of the Mojave desert.

I didn't have any idea what Twentynine Palms held in store but I did know what Camp Pendleton represented and I was glad to get what I did. Orders to report to Pendleton were the same as a ticket to Vietnam with a strong possibility that it would be a one-way affair. Little did I know that my safe ride to the desert would translate into a boat ride to Chulai in less than four months' time.

The most humorous assignment was Private Ward's. He was

to report to some remote outpost in Alaska. Most of the men in the platoon were from Minnesota and there was general agreement that the sub-zero temperatures and heavy snow were things to be avoided if at all possible. Ward was unhappy about going to a place where the climate was even worse than Minnesota but accepted his lot with a look of sheepish resignation.

Sgt. Barton gave us fifteen minutes to digest our orders and talk them over with the rest of the turds. Most of the privates who were going to Camp Pendleton were acting very proud of themselves and claimed to be the true marines in the platoon. They agreed that they must have shown themselves to be the toughest privates in boot camp because they had gotten the toughest assignments. Someone pointed out that the tests which were used as the basis for the orders were given to us in the first week of training so it was obvious that the dumbest ones in the bunch were made into grunts.

The discussion grew more heated and noisy and several privates, acting from their newly acquired identities as marine infantrymen, were getting ready to solve the argument with old-fashioned fisticuffs.

The DI told us to fall in on the street and marched us over to the sand. If we wanted to make a bunch of goddam noise instead of acting like men he'd treat us the same way that we treated him. We had shown no respect for his eardrums so he was just forced to take care of us and teach us a little manners.

We thrashed in the rain until dark.

CHAPTER FOURTEEN

The Cat only grinned when it saw Alice. It looked good-natured, she thought: still it had very long claws and a great many teeth, so she felt it ought to be treated with respect.

One morning, immediately after breakfast, we were brought to a remote corner of the base and put in the bleachers. There seemed to be bleachers in the oddest spots around that base.

We were waiting for something to happen when a creature popped out from behind a tree. With a second look we recognized it as a human being, though the distinction was not great. He was wearing rags that were camouflaged to blend in with the trees, and the parts of his body that weren't covered by the rags were painted black and several shades of green.

He walked closer to us and we could see a bald, painted head and a face with a huge moustache that was made to look like part of the camouflage. It was our old friend Sergeant Fox. He looked as if he had spent a month alone in the woods with no equipment.

He gave a bow that was half drama and half elegance and smiled brightly. "Good morning, Privates," he said.

"Good morning, sir."

"The smoking lamp is lit for one cigarette."

"Sir, the smoking lamp is lit for one cigarette, aye, aye, sir."

"Privates, this morning we are going to discuss survival. I will tell you straight away that not a single one of you has ever been in a position where the main thing that you needed to do above all else was survive.

"I'm not talking about making it through Central Park after dark, I'm talking about being alone in the jungle; cut off from all normal means of support and not having any idea how long you'll be there or which way to travel in order to get back to safety. I'm referring to what would happen if you should ever become separated from your unit in Vietnam."

He ordered his assistant to bring in some props and set them on the table in front of us.

"If, by some unfortunate twist of fate, you should ever get lost, you must know what to do in order to survive what could prove to be a very tough time." He paused and looked at us.

"The first thing you must do is avoid capture. If you get caught by the VC, God help you," he said.

He then went into a demonstration of how to disguise oneself using only the materials that one would find growing in the jungle. He showed us how to avoid villages, how to read the land to find drinkable water, which types of terrain to use and which to avoid; and why, and how to find our way back to friendly territory. "So the first and most important thing to do is avoid capture and find your way home," he repeated.

"In the meantime you must find ways to supply your basic needs. These are mainly shelter and food." He showed us the various types of shelters that could be constructed in case of emergency. We learned how to set the shelters up and dismantle them without leaving a trace for the enemy to find.

Toward the end of the class he put us back in the bleachers. He seemed to have no limit on the amount of happiness he could extract from his work and his energetic enthusiasm had us all in the same frame of mind.

The instructor's assistant brought him a cage containing a large, fluffy, white rabbit. Sgt. Fox took the docile animal from the cage and held it in the crook of his left arm while he stroked it gently with his right hand. He talked soothingly into the bunny's ear as if it were an old and dear pet.

"Let us assume," he said, "that you are very clever and

126

manage to catch an animal like my friend Peter here. Let us also assume that you have in your possession a knife of some sort."

The rabbit was half asleep as Sgt. Fox caressed the nape of his neck and scratched under his chin. He said something to his friend Peter about "showing the privates our trick." He held the rabbit's hind legs and let him fall forward until he was stretched out full length with his head down and his front feet kicking to regain his balance.

The Sgt. held the bunny up for us to see and hit it with a hammer-like karate chop in the back of the neck that he had been caressing just moments before. He grinned and waved the dead animal at us before flopping it down on the table.

He pulled out his knife and said cheerfully, "Step one," and sliced the rabbit's head off with one hard stroke. "Step two,"—he slit the carcass from throat to anus. "Step three,"—he pulled the entrails out and threw them aside. He wiped his bloody hands on the rabbit's fur.

"Next," he said, "you cut around each leg, like so, and...roll his sleeves down. Cut off the feet like this, put one in your pocket for luck and throw the other three in the waste pile. Then you just grab here by the shoulders and peel the hide right off.

He held up the pitifully skinny remains of the formerly fluffy Peter Rabbit. "You then wash out the meat and roast it over a small fire. Did everybody get that?" he asked.

"Yes, sir," we answered with one voice.

"Good. When you have finished dining you must always remember to bury your fire along with all the scraps." He scraped everything into a bloody pile. "Except for this," he said, picking out the red and white blood-drenched fur. "Since you are all alone and will undoubtly desire some friendly company out there in the jungle"...he fitted the rabbit fur over his hand and formed a puppet out of it.

"Hi, Peter," he said to the puppet, "nice to see you again."

"Hi, Sarge," the puppet squeaked back, "nice to see you."

The bleachers rocked with laughter. The outburst was partly relief from the tension of the gory exhibition that we had

127

witnessed and partly because it was just plain funny.

Sgt. Fox and Peter waved and walked back behind the tree from which he had originally emerged.

We fell out and marched to lunch.

After lunch we returned to survival class, ready for more of Sgt. Fox's antics.

He was still outfitted in his jungle suit when he came out to start the class. He gave us the usual exuberant greeting and started right out with an explanation of poisonous and non-poisonous plants, how to spot and avoid booby traps, and how to travel across rivers and streams safely. We had more practical application and the afternoon passed quickly.

For the grand finale Sgt. Fox had another cage brought out which contained a very large green and yellow snake with hooded eyes. The instructor told us it was not dangerous but I wasn't entirely sure that everyone believed him. The snake moved with slow, sinewy power and his eyes radiated wary slyness. I would have avoided any type of contact with it if at all possible. Venomous or not, it looked like a formidable opponent to me.

The instructor hauled the snake out of the cage and held it just below its thick neck while it wrapped its five-foot length around the Sgt.'s arm several times.

"Now the essence of all that I have been trying to teach you privates is this," he said, ignoring the attempts of the snake to escape. "In order to survive in the jungle environment you must first and foremost have the will to live. You must assume a frame of mind that is beyond fear, beyond panic, and beyond the most basic weakness of man: the tendency to give up hope when faced with what appears to be an overwhelming setting."

"Now listen up," he said. "What seems to be real is very often the projection of what's in the mind into the environment. In other words we tend to cover reality with our own expectations and fears and lose sight of what really is. Take this snake here. If we project what's in our minds onto the snake and more or less 'coat' him with fear he will be more dangerous to us. That is the nature of the jungle and that's what's going to determine whether you live or die. If you 'coat' the jungle with your own fear or hopelessness you will give up and die. If you see the jungle, or the snake, as it really is, you have an excellent chance to survive. Know the basic characteristics of the environment, follow sensible rules, and it will work out fine." He shook his fingers at us, "but above all, you must have an overpowering will to live.

He stopped and looked at the snake. "Let's say that you have no weapons, you can't build a fire, and you've gotten your hands on a little beauty like this. You could wish for a knife, you could wait for the snake to starve to death before you did, or you could.......

SURVIVE!!!!"

He jammed the head of the snake into his mouth and bit it off with one violent crunch! I couldn't believe it! He spit the head out and held the squirming, twisting reptile up for us to look at. Blood poured from the gaping wound and flowed down over the instructor's arm, splattering on his face and body. The dead snake gave up its futile attempt to find its head and went limp except for intermittent twitches of dying nerves.

Sgt. Fox, his face, chest, and arm mottled with blood, gave us a serious stare. He was breathing hard.

"Do you get the idea?" he shouted, casting the snake into the dust.

"Yes, sir," we answered quietly, stunned by what he had done.

"DO YOU GET THE IDEA?!" he shouted more vehemently.

"YES, SIR," we shouted back.

"Fine. I truly hope that not a man-jack here will ever find it necessary to use this information. If you do, please remember what you have been taught today. Good day, privates."

"Good day, sir," we answered.

He nodded, smiled through the blood on his mouth, spun on his heel, and stalked off.

❧   ❧   ❧

June, 1966
Near Huë City, S. Vietnam

The word came down from Battalion that we weren't getting enough bodies for the daily count. The people on the top end of the chain of command were putting the pressure on to step up our activities and increase the number of kills so that the war could be ended.

By this time we knew that Charlie was a stronger and fiercer enemy than anyone had ever dreamed when we first landed in 'Nam. We had a standing joke that Charlie could go on losing a lot longer then we could go on winning.

Only about half of us were original members of C company. The rest had been killed, or wounded and sent home, or managed to work their way into safe details. The newer replacements were anxious to seek out Charlie and when the word came down that we had to increase patrols the young guys became eager volunteers, thus freeing up the rest of us from having to do it. The time had long since passed when we had any desire to save face or keep up appearances and so we were quite content to let the new guys do their thing. The officers insisted on always having at least two or three old hands on every patrol so we worked out an elaborate schedule that allowed the maximum time off for each person in the short-timers' pool.

Despite the caution and wiliness that we developed toward the end of our tours some of the short-timers still got greased. It was a frustrating and painful time. Whenever a guy who was short got nailed the rest of us seemed to get depressed and bitchy for two or three days. We had gotten to the point where we recognized the futility and utter waste of the war and it was extremely hard to accept the fact that one of the "boys" was zapped after skipping through for so long.

One of the most outspoken guys in the "club" was Tom Eisenhower. Ike was getting antiwar literature in the mail regularly and openly passed it on to the rest of us. We would smoke grass and discuss the pros and cons of our situation while we read Ike's mail. Nothing was ever resolved in our discussions because we all agreed that regardless of right or wrong, good or bad, the one thing we all wanted was to get out of the country and go home. We did nothing to subvert the effort of the U.S.

130

but we did as much as possible to avoid getting fucked up by Chuck and his booby traps.

When Lt. Lang came to C company he was quickly convinced that the short-timers' club was an undermining element that was destroying the company's morale. Unlike the experienced officers he would not turn his head the other way when he saw us using pot or gathering to rap about how to stay alive. He made it his personal business to straighten us out. What he didn't realize was that we were the most reliable troops, when it came to actual combat, that he could possibly have hoped for. We knew what we were doing and we were very good at it.

Lt. Lang decided that Ike was the main culprit in the club and he promised to "hang" him. The Lt. started sending him out on every possible patrol and even made up his own operations without the CO's knowledge in an effort to break Eisenhower's spirit and bring what he considered order into the company.

The rest of us did what we could to see to it that Ike didn't get an unfair deal. When we started volunteering for his assignments the Lt. disallowed it.

Ike was starting to crack under the strain. His eyes took on the eerie glow that usually preceded a total crack-up.

One morning we awoke to the sharp explosion of a grenade. It was followed by two rifle shots, then silence. When the smoke cleared Lt. Lang lay dead, riddled with hundreds of pieces of shrapnel and two bullets in the head. His body had been smashed so badly that it was barely recognizable. Ribbons of smoke curled up from the dead form.

Ike was squatting like a gook ten feet from the body, staring at his dead leader, a grin like a diabolical cat splitting his face.

He was led away by the CO and he never quit grinning. After several months of psychiatric care he was court-martialed and sentenced to death by firing squad. The sentence was commuted life imprisonment in Portsmouth, where he will remain, doing hard labor, until he dies.

CHAPTER FIFTEEN

"At any rate I'll never go there again!" said Alice as she picked her way through the wood. "It's the stupidest tea party I ever was at in all my life!"

For the last few weeks of training we were given a new drill instructor to replace Cpl. Torres. The new Sgt.'s name was Lofgren. He worked with one of the main DIs most of the time at first and then was gradually allowed to take over by himself for twenty-four periods. We thought he was a new DI just breaking in to his first platoon because he was an entirely different type of person than Sgt. Barton or Sgt. Liebermann.

He was tall and thin with smallish features and a pale complexion and even though he carried himself proudly and militarily erect, he just did not have the same kind of violent aura about him that the other ones had.

When Sgt. Lofgren was on duty it was downright pleasant in comparison to a normal day of training. He only raised his voice when it was absolutely necessary and he rarely punished us on a whim. If we did something as outrageous as talk when at attention or something equally as ridiculous he would not hesitate to work us over but all in all he was very fair and mild. He allowed us four or five minutes for a shit call instead of the usual two, he lit the lamp after every meal and before taps, and he would actually sit in the evening and talk with us as human beings.

A lot of emphasis was being placed on polishing up our drilling because we were supposed to have our final inspection and drill competition at the tail end of training. Private Jones was still having difficulty with some of the more complex maneuvers and nothing seemed to work as far as getting him to understand it. After an exasperating day on the grinder Sgt. Lofgren took us back to platoon street and had us clean our rifles. He took Private Jones out on the grinder and went over the steps of the drill with him. We could see him patiently coaching Jones, walking through it with him and standing back to watch as Jones went through the steps alone. Time after time Jones made mistakes and each time the DI would explain how to do it all over again. After an hour Jones was still making errors but he was doing better than ever before. Sgt. Lofgren took Jones out every evening for a week, even coming back on his time off, and calmly went over the drill steps with him. When the week was up Jones could do a fairly acceptable version of close order drill.

For us to witness a drill instructor displaying patience and understanding to a turd was a minor miracle. We started to look forward eagerly to the days when the benign DI would be on duty and we grew to consider them a day of respite. I began to think that maybe the service wasn't going to be too bad after all if there were a lot of people like him running it.

Sgt. Liebermann had duty one day and Sgt. Lofgren was assisting him. They marched us to the base exchange so that we could replenish our supply of hygiene gear and other necessary items. When we got back to platoon street Sgt. Liebermann did not dismiss as we expected. Instead, to the grief of several privates, he had us empty our grocery bags at our feet and step back from them. Fortunately for me and most of the platoon we had not purchased any contraband. Unfortunately for them, seven turds stood in front of neat little piles of candy, bought at the exchange and smuggled past the DIs as they stood at the door waiting for us to finish shopping.

"So we got some goddam sugar lovers here, eh? You goddam

pukey maggots smuggled pogey bait into my platoon street. The rest of you turds put your gear away, the sugar lovers bring your candy up to me."

We put our things away and returned to the street in time to watch the seven smugglers eat their candy. Sgt. Liebermann did not allow them to remove the wrappings. One private choked on the paper and vomited and then had to pick the half paper-clad candy from the puke and put it back in his mouth.

I happened to look at Sgt. Lofgren while the banquet was in session and I caught a distinct look of disapproval. It was apparent that he did not agree with Sgt. Liebermann. He was attempting to remain neutral but did a poor job of hiding his sensitivity and sympathy for the privates. He was far too profes-sional to intervene, of course, but nonetheless it was obvious to me what he was thinking.

Gary Scriver was also the happy recipient of Sgt. Lofgren's even temperament. Somehow, as wildly impossible as it seemed, Scriver had managed to get in contact with a woman who was stationed at the base for a school and he had snuck out at night several times to meet her for a sexual liaison.

The rule about leaving the quonset huts at night was that if a private had to make a head call he could do so, but had to go out wearing undershirt, trousers and shower shoes.

Scriver was found by Sgt. Lofgren three blocks from the platoon street wearing his full uniform with his top button undone as if he was a marine stationed at the base. Only recruits who graduated that day were allowed to wear the top of the shirt open and under no circumstances could a recruit walk around like that. Gary was caught red-handed. He readily admitted to the DI what he was doing and told the whole story with the exception of the girl's name.

If anyone other than Sgt. Lofgren had caught him Scriver would at least have been fined heavily and made to grovel in the sand for a long time. For some unexplainable reason the DI merely sent him back to the barracks after a hundred push-ups. Scriver did not attempt any more late night forays when

Sgt. Lofgren was on duty. What threats of imprisonment and mayhem could not even touch, leniency had conquered completely.

When Private Scriver turned over a new leaf and stopped haunting the base at night he included only the nights when Sgt. Lofgren was on duty. When one of the other drill instructor's was there Scriver considered his resolution null and void.

He needed someone to share his clandestine adventures with so he picked me because he knew I could be trusted to keep intact the confidentiality that was a necessary part of the midnight runs. The only catch was that I didn't think it either wise or healthy to get involved in something that would land me in the brig. I had already been to see the old man once for being AWOL and going to see him again would be the end of me as a member of Platoon 211. I certainly didn't have any great love or loyalty or emotional dependence on the platoon. The only consideration was that 211 was going to graduate from basic training in short order and I didn't know of any brig rats that would be leaving sooner. I turned Scriver's offer down with an emphatic no. He asked me at least twice a day and I still said no.

During the evening free time he buttonholed me and said that tonight would be the best party he had set up so far. I said I wasn't interested.

"Well," he said slyly, "I guess I'll just have to take care of both of them."

I knew he was up to no good but couldn't resist. "Both of who?"

"Aw, don't worry about it, Dan, I'll handle it all right."

"Both of who, Scriver, goddam you?" He had me.

"Both of the chicks I lined us up with tonight," he said airily, dismissing the subject with a wave of his hand and appearing to lapse into thought. He shook his head sadly. "That one Alice chick is sure a sweet little fox...," he trailed off again trying to figure out a way to handle the situation later on.

"OK Gary, out with it. What's going on? What's this Alice bullshit?"

He looked at me to see if the bait was completely set. He

whispered quickly, "They're waiting for us. Are you in or out?"

I swallowed. "I'm in."

His pupils widened with triumph and he smiled happily. "We'll leave a half hour after taps."

I was wavering already and he saw it.

"Don't worry." He punched me lightly. "It's foolproof."

The DI got us out on the street for roll call and sent us back inside the huts for lights out. As the barracks went dark and the sounds of Taps played over the base I had an attack of butterflies in the stomach.

A sharp stab of desire dismissed the nervousness as the minutes ticked away. I was sitting on a keg of sexual gunpowder that I was more than willing to let explode if the opportunity presented itself and the conversation that I had with Scriver had lit the fuse. I was ready to go.

All the other turds in my hut were sound asleep when the back door creaked. I got out of my rack silently and stuffed the pillow under the covers to make it look as though someone was sleeping there if one of the DIs happened to look in. I saw that done in a movie once. I dressed swiftly and walked over to the door and peeked out to make certain it was Gary. He was standing there as if he was waiting in line at a supermarket or somewhere equally casual. I saw that his top button was undone like the regular marines on the base and unbuttoned mine as I slipped out the door.

He waved for me to follow him. In thirty seconds we were out of the platoon area and strolling along the edge of the parade field. Scriver made a series of turns, cut across a couple of open fields, and soon I lost all sense of where we were and where we were going. He knew the base like his own backyard and we walked along his chosen route without so much as seeing a guard or causing attention to be drawn to us in any form. After about fifteen minutes of walking we came to a lightly wooded area at the edge of a football field and paused for a moment. When he was satisfied that the coast was clear he led me to a vine-covered fence that we followed until we came to a small building. Scriver reached in his pocket and pulled out a key which he used to unlock the door. We went in and stood silently in the darkness.

When our eyes became accustomed to the light he showed me a stack of sweatshirts and indicated that we should cover the two windows with them. We managed to rig up some light-stopping curtains, find the switch and turn the lights on. The building that we were illegally occupying was an equipment shack for the base football team. I speculated for a couple of seconds on the general's reaction to two turds burglarizing his team's shop.

"We're not gonna get caught," my friend said with a grin, "so just relax and enjoy yourself."

I decided he was right and sat down to bite my nails rather than standing up to bite them. I did manage to relax shortly.

My heart jumped when someone rapped softly on the door. Gary went over and opened it. He invited our dates in with an elegant bow and sweeping motion of the hand. They came through the entrance giggling.

I was introduced as Don Renner to the girls who were named Alice and Patty. Knowing Scriver as I did I was not at all surprised to hear them refer to him as Johnny. I caught his wink.

Alice was rather plain, she was about five feet four inches tall, had brown hair, blue eyes, and a slim figure. She was my date for the evening. Patty was fat with red hair and a wide mouth that jumped off her face. For some mysterious reason she was perfect for Scriver in a setting like that.

"Well, well, well, what are the naughty recruits doing out so late at night?," Patty said with a huge smile.

I didn't have any idea how to answer the question so Scriver said, "You know your little Johnny just can't stay away from you, sweetheart. Even us turds need some lovin' now and then." He squeezed the oversized cheek of her ass and smiled charmingly. Patty giggled, rolled her brown eyeballs up, and snuck a quick peek at her girl friend to see if she had caught the romantic exchange that took place.

I said to Alice, "Um...would you like to sit down?" She

glanced around at the football gear trying to find a chair, of which we happened to be fresh out. "No, thanks, Don," she said. I tried again. "I'm sorry I can't offer you a drink."

"Oh, that's ok." She smiled politely.

"So...uh...do you like the Marines?," I said.

"It's not bad."

"Well, that's good...." I was starting to sweat. I had just about run out of cute things to say and it didn't look as though Alice was going to originate anything particularly brilliant. "We could sit on the floor," I said, indicating the floor.

"All right."

We sat down on the floor and I studied my hands while she pawed through her purse looking for a cigarette. It was not going well at all. We managed to start talking about her job as a personnel clerk and passed the time that way while I plotted and schemed and made mental pictures of sweeping her into my arms in a passionate embrace. We ran out of things that were interesting about her job and there was another period of silence while we both racked our brains to think of something to say.

The silence was periodically punctured by a giggle from Patty and a groan or two from "Johnny." They were in the back of the room behind a row of lockers.

"I brought some cards," Alice said brightly.

"Why don't we make love instead?" I blurted out. I could feel my face getting hot as soon as I said it.

Alice looked down and then started going through her purse again, this time for the deck of cards. She gave me her best look of primness and said, "I don't do that sort of thing on the first date." She went back to her search.

I was relieved that at least I had broached the subject and said to her, "No offense."

She got serious. "I'm not offended. Really I'm not. I realize that men have stronger drives than women and that you don't need any emotional involvement to have affairs." It sounded as if she was recruiting something from memory. "In our basic training we had sexual hygiene classes to learn to understand

139

situations like this so I want you to know that I do understand and I don't want you to feel embarrassed for asking." End of quote.

I didn't know what to make of it so I said, "Ok, let's just play cards."

"Maybe next time," she said clinically and patted my cheek.

I was ready to let the romance part of the date go as a lost cause and was glad to see her find the cards.

We played hearts and waited for Scriver and his girl friend to come out from their love nest.

Scriver started to fuck his fat lover. I could hear the slapping noises and moans and periodically a loud grunt would escape Patty's ample mouth.

I thought it was funny and had to suppress my laughter. It was the first time I ever heard the sounds of sex. Alice played her hand as if nothing was going on, being very careful not to get any more hearts than necessary.

I had a wild urge to let a fart. A loud, wet fart would suit the situation perfectly, I thought, laughing to myself. I wished that we had had cabbage and beer for supper.

The noise died down in the rear of the shack and before very long the two lovers came out into the light. Patty was rumpled and had a dreamy look on her face as she cast grateful eyes at Scriver. He was also messed up and the look in his eyes showed that he was finished with that caper and thinking about the next.

We talked for a while and then the girls decided it was time to get back to their rooms. They got up to depart.

Alice pecked me on the cheek and said, "Thanks for a good time." Patty gave Scriver a long, meaningful kiss and told him to leave a note when he could get away again. They went out after Gary checked to see if it was safe.

When the girls had gone Scriver slapped me on the back and beamed, "How'd you make out sport?"

"Maybe next time. Let's get the hell out of here."

We arranged the building so that it was the same as when we

came. The route we followed on the way back was different from the original way because, according to Private Scriver, there was a rearrangement of the guard at midnight.

We got back to the barracks without mishap. I got inside and ducked my head back out. Scriver was moving like a silent shadow back toward the parade grounds. He was off on another scheme.

I got into the safety of my bunk and vowed that I would stay put until boot camp was over. Breaking rocks for thirty days as punishment for playing hearts was not my idea of fun.

CHAPTER SIXTEEN

"Cheshire Puss," she began, rather timidly..., "Would you tell me, please, which way I ought to walk from here?"

"That depends a good deal on where you want to get to," said the Cat.

"I don't much care where—" said Alice.

"Then it doesn't matter which way you walk," said the Cat.

"—so long as I get somewhere, *" Alice added as an explanation.*

"Oh, you're sure to do that," said the Cat, "if you only walk long enough."

Alice felt that this could not be denied, so she tried another question. "What sort of people live about here?"

"In that direction," the Cat said, waving its right paw round, "lives a Hatter; and in that direction," waving the other paw, "lives a March Hare. Visit either you like: they're both mad."

"But I don't want to go among mad people," Alice remarked.

"Oh, you can't help that," said the Cat: "we're all mad here. I'm mad. You're mad."

"How do you know I'm mad?" said Alice.

"You must be," said the Cat, "or you wouldn't have come here."

In the final days of boot camp we shifted to an intense regimen of classes on Marine Corps history and tradition. All the tests had been passed and barring some major catastrophe we were assured of graduating on schedule.

To turn us out without finishing off our mental conditioning would have meant that quite a few privates would leave without acquiring the "esprit de corps" that was a major part of the DI's objective. The obvious solution to the problem was to show us just what it was that we were about to become a part of.

We had hour after hour of classes. In them we learned what the Marines had been doing since the Revolutionary War.

We learned that the Corps was formed on tenth November, 1775 at a place called Tun Tavern in Philadelphia. They served in the War for Independence and then dwindled and disappeared.

On July 11, 1798 the U.S. Marine Corps offically came into existence. In the year 1800 the Marines made their first landing in the Dominican Republic. From the time of their introduction to battle in 1800 until the mid-1930's the Marines made armed invasions of foreign countries on over 125 separate occasions. As the instructor proudly pointed out, the Marines became the symbol of Yankee Imperialism and Might to countries all over the world, from China to Africa to France to Russia.

"The Marine Corps has kicked ass and taken names from one end of this globe to the other, privates!" our instructor was fond of repeating.

We learned that in the 1830's the Commandant of the Marine Corps, Archibald Henderson, volunteered his services to the President for the purpose of aiding in the Seminole Indian War. Shortly before that war the area of Florida was owned by the government of Spain. For many years negro slaves who had escaped captivity found refuge with the Seminoles and gradually intermarried with members of the tribe. The southern plantation owners made pleas to the Spanish government for the return of their property and when their petitions came to naught the slave traders and owners put pressure on the U.S. government to buy a part of Florida. The government did so, and took the Seminoles under its wing to protect them from the slavers. When the U.S. promptly turned its head and the slave trading began in earnest the Seminoles fought back. This went on for about ten years and then the government decided to transport the Indians to a reservation in Arkansas. When the Indians resisted the Army was sent in to force the Seminoles to move. The Army had no luck with the stubborn Indians so the Marines were called in. Working as a team the Army and Marines set up concentration camps near New Orleans to hold the Indians. In 1842, seven years after the Marines entered Florida, the war petered out and the Marines returned north. Some 4,000 Seminoles moved to Oklahoma and the rest escaped from the concentration camps and melted back into the swamps. Although the Marines did not win, and did not lose, valuable experience had been gained.

The Marines invaded Cuba to protect American sugar investments; Nicaragua to protect railroad investments; Haiti to protect extensive investments by American, French, and German entrepreneurs, and more than a dozen other countries to maintain the governments that the U.S. considered advantageous.

As the classes went on and I learned more about how the U.S. had manipulated the governments of dozens upon dozens of foreign countries I became confused about just exactly what the government that I had sworn to uphold represented. During my school days I learned that the U.S. is a peace-loving country that became involved in war only when it was absoutely necessary to survive. I never conceived—or even considered it possible—that our government had been meddling in the affairs of foreign countries since a few short years after its birth as a nation. It came as a surprise to find out that we had been at war more than we had been in a state of peace during all that time.

I shrugged my shoulders at the paradox and concentrated on learning the information in case a drill instructor happened to ask me a question about it. Knowing the facts as they were given out by the instructors was far more important than whether or not the history books I had studied in school were truthful. I didn't have the time to get caught up in trying to make a decision about the morality of the history of either the Marine Corps or the U.S. government. It was disturbing to know that money interests in the U.S. and its allied countries were a very important factor in our past foreign policy and that we had been determining the fate of foreign governments almost continually, but, since it was necessary and even dangerous to question our past activities, I simply learned what I was told to learn.

When the relatively dry history lessons were over the instructors began giving classes on highlights of Marine battles and told stories of the legendary heroes whose shoes we would be trying to fill. As the hours flew by the platoon slowly grew proud of the Corps. Inspired by the ghosts of Chesty Puller and John Basilone, Smedley Butler and Dan Daly, and many others who exemplified the spirit of the Marines we went to bed each night and dreamed of honor and glory.

The training we received was the same as all the great marines who stood out above the average man. We had the same training as Sgt. John Quick, the Spanish-American War hero. Sgt. Quick's platoon was set up on a hill, behind a blockhouse defended by Spanish troops, for the purpose of cutting off any chance of retreat when the main force of Marines attacked the blockhouse from the front. Just before the frontal assualt began naval gunfire support was called for. The barrage laid down by the USS *Dolphin* was a little too high and the shells landed on the Marine platoon. With an arrogant disdain for his own safety Sgt. Quick improvised a signal flag and stood in full view of the enemy. As the bullets of the Spanish soldiers and the heavy shells of the Navy tore the air and erupted all around him Sgt. Quick calmly signaled the *Dolphin* to cease fire. The barrage lifted and the Marines were able to attack the blockhouse. Although outnumbered by six companies to two the Marines routed the enemy, who later reported that they had been attacked by what they thought was 10,000 Marines. Sgt. Quick was awarded the Medal of Honor and a prominent place in subsequent recruit classes.

Not all of the classes were about individual marines. Some were about units of the Corps made up of ordinary marines like the turds of 211. We heard the story of Iwo Jima, where 5,931 marines were killed and 17,272 were wounded in thirty-six days of hand-to-hand fighting. Every last Japanese defender—save a handful of badly wounded prisoners—was wiped out, 21,000 in all. Ira Hayes helped raise the flag in the most famous photograph ever taken of combat. The average, everyday marine was the one who had taken Iwo and caused Fleet Admiral Nimitz to remark, "Uncommon valor was a common virtue."

Guadalcanal, Tarawa, Saipan, Tinian, Guam, and Okinawa were glorious moments in Marine history that were replayed for us in detail. We saw on film and heard first-hand from some of the survivors who had been there of the unprecedented savagery and courage of the Marine assaults. We saw and heard and believed.

We were told of the Chosin Reservoir in Korea. The First Marine Division, while advancing north on the communist positions, was surrounded by the Chinese Ninth Army Group —a ten-division force sent to Korea for the specific purpose of destroying the 1st Division. When General Oliver Smith was warned that the division was outnumbered ten to one in the reservoir he ordered the unit to fight its way back to the ocean, some seventy miles southeast.

Press correspondents asked the General if he was ordering the Marines to retreat, an almost unheard of situation. "Gentlemen," he replied, "the Marine Corps does not retreat. We are just attacking in a different direction."

The Marines smashed out of the circle of Chinese troops and began an epic march to the sea, taking their dead and their equipment along with them. During the thirteen-day march to Hungnam, the port of debarkation, the Marines were surrounded and broke out uncounted times. In the freezing winds and searing cold they marched and fought. Cooks and mechanics became riflemen, and instead of boiling potatoes or changing spark plugs they found themselves using bayonets and M1 rifles to save their own lives and take the lives of the Chinese.

Although the temperature reached twenty-four degrees below zero, and most of the men had frozen feet, the First Division staggered on to its destination, leaving no one behind except dead Chinese. When the. division reached Hungnam it had completed a breakout unparalleled in military history. While suffering 4,400 combat losses and 7,000 losses to the bitter cold, the Marines inflicted such devastating casualties on the Chinese communist force that they could not operate as a military organization for several months. Of the original ten enemy divisions, specially trained and organized for the purpose of destroying marines, only three remained. The First Division was back in action in just over three weeks.

Much emphasis was placed on the Marines' superior ability as combat troops and many examples were given of the Marines taking hills after the Army failed, the Marines standing up and repulsing massive enemy attacks while some other lesser breed of soldier buckled, and the Marines volunteering for missions that other groups dared not even think of attempting.

The degradation of boot training slowly faded as the pride that was our heritage came to the fore. All but a handful of the privates went through the final days with eyes shining, backs straight, and minds glued to the future battles in Vietnam.

I found myself rationalizing about recruit training and the slaughter of war. I almost believed it possible to stand up in front of a horde of assaulting gooks with a bayonet and pluck, smashing the enemy to the ground with the help of the spirits of past marines. It was much harder to resist the glory and color that flowed down through the ages than it was to fight against the dismantling of self that had been going on for eleven weeks.

The one thing that kept me from accepting the "esprit de corps" that the classes were intended to impart was the thought that for every hero who lived to receive his crown of glory there were thousands of men who had died whimpering in the dirt, unable to hold their own shit back because their wounds were so horrible. I knew instinctively that the admiration was for the heroes, but for the blind and crippled there was only darkness and people trying not to stare.

❧   ❧   ❧

September, 1968

When it finally happened it came totally unexpected.

There were only three months left on my second tour of duty in 'Nam. How I got there the second time is a long story involv-

148

ing a court-martial and inability to tolerate the whims and personality traits of the officers and NCOs in a noncombat setting. That story is better left untold for now. At any rate there were only three months to go and I had managed, by acting crazy (I put an orange scarf over my eyes and told my leaders over and over, until they believed me, that I was a carrot and would they please allow me to grow in peace?) to get myself placed in a radio outfit at a small airfield just south of the DMZ.

I was in a deep, pot-induced sleep when the rockets and mortars started screaming down on top of us. Oddly enough I slept through the first explosions that took place right outside the door of my hootch and the burning chunks of shrapnel passed through the thin plywood wall and over my prostrate body. On the second round, a few seconds later, I jumped up and ran, buck-assed naked, to the nearest bunker. Two steps from the sandbagged opening I felt the concussion of a sixty-millimeter mortar slam against my left side. I staggered once and ducked into the darkness of the bunker. In ten seconds my whole upper torso felt as though it had been seared with a white hot poker. I started feeling with my right hand, frantically groping in the dark to find out if I had anything left on the side of my body at all. I kept poking with my right hand and repeating "eighty-seven, eighty-seven, eighty-seven"—the number of days remaining until I was due to rotate back to the U.S. A couple of the guys stretched me out on the dirt and someone produced a flashlight.

You're ok, man, it's just your shoulder, you lucky bastard. You'll be getting the fuck outta here now," somebody said.

I had an enormous desire to give the man a dissertation on how this was my nineteenth month in-country and I had just 87 stinkin' lousy fucking days to do and I'd be getting out of the fuckin' rathole anyway, so how did that add up to being lucky? I said nothing.

The pain localized in the left shoulder when the panic left. The barrage lifted and someone came for me in a jeep. I dressed, climbed in the back and accidentally sat on Louie Antonelli, the fat little cook. He was dead. I adjusted myself and we went to the medical bunker.

Outside the bunker a group of guys were stacking the dead on a large truck. There wasn't enough room for everyone so some of the dead had to spend their final truck ride jammed on top of some other snuffee. I thought that at least the asshole driver would have the courtesy to make two trips.

When the doc got around to me he was tired and fed up with the whole thing. I wanted to ask him to get a little shut-eye before he got the scalpel out but I didn't want to piss him off more so I let it pass. He gave me a shot of novocaine, opened the arm up a little and cleaned up the mess inside. In a matter of thirty minutes I was back in my hootch.

For three days I walked around doing nothing but smoke pot and visit with my friends. On the fourth day I opened the bandage a bit to see how the small holes were healing and the odor almost dropped me to my knees. I had neglected to go to sick bay for cleaning and the thing was rotting in the moist heat. It was more than badly infected.

When the doc saw my arm he started cursing and threatened me with a court-martial for destruction of government property. "You dumb son-of-a-bitch, are you ever gonna learn to take an order and execute it like a man? There's nothing I can do for you now. I'm sending you to Japan for surgery, and for your sake I hope they can save your fucking arm!" I took it for granted that he was overacting like some of the fools who passed for officers and I went back to the hootch for my things.

After a quick stop at the Commanding Officer's tent, where I was busted from Lance Corporal to PFC for disobeying an order, I went by jeep to the Army hospital about five miles south.

I spent two days there, getting the black skin removed and being poked in the ass with huge penicillin-charged needles every four hours. A regimen of painkilling hypos was also started and I made sure that each time it was due I got my fair share of the soothing drug.

I was medevaced by helicopter. As the chopper pulled up into the sky I was treated to a sweeping view of the countryside that I hated and loved at the same time. Vietnam is so stunningly beautiful in places that I felt as though I could embrace it with my whole heart and soul. The trouble was that a tangible aura of decay and sorrow and pain gripped the place with a fierce and unyielding fist.

The wind rushed in the open doorway that framed the green-clad machine gunner and his tool, the M-60. Looking beyond the figure of the gunner I could see miles of green jungle, uninhabited and totally unexplored in places. There were huge hills, wrapped in a blue haze of humidity and thousands of acres of water-covered rice paddies that reflected the bright sun and gave lie to the idea that this was a violent country. We made a hard right turn and the chopper banked toward the South China Sea. At the steepest point in the turn I could see the shadow of our helicopter on the ground hundreds of feet below. We were swooping smoothly and swiftly over an elaborate graveyard. I felt a roar of happiness that I was not one of the unseeing denizens that populated the brightly decorated and icily real cemetery. I was on my way home.

like food and drink to Sgt. Barton and he responded to the stimulus with a vibrancy and color that put him on a higher plane than the competing platoon commanders of 210 and 212.

As the drill instructor went so went the platoon. We were so dependent on the DI's direction after weeks of receiving orders to do even the most mundane and trivial tasks that we were like putty in his hands. We warmed to the drill in direct ratio to Sgt. Barton's enthusiasm and by the time we were a third of the way through it our movements had become so sharply even and delicately smooth that we were the winners of final drill and thus the honor platoon. That realization served as fuel for the fire that we felt.

We finished the drill with rifle movements. Spinning, tossing, clicking and slapping with one sound, always one sound, we ended our display with a flourish. Each squad was doing a different yet related exercise and Sgt. Barton, platoon commander extraordinaire, was coordinating all of our activities at the same time. Like a master magician, burning with the zeal of his calling, the DI shouted out orders as if he was pulling an endless array of silk scarves from his sleeve. At the peak of his performance he was part circus barker and part Shakespearean actor, formal in tone and demeanor yet colorfully creative in result. Like a High Priest of whirling dervishes that dashed and strutted and reacted to his every command, he spurred us on to show a competence that we were not even aware we were capable of.

We finished and marched off the field like conquering heroes, the magnitude of our certain victory firmly established in our minds.

The other platoons gave excellent but less impressive and more low-key showings.

After the drill we stood another inspection that was basically the same as the one we had at the three-week mark of our training. The one difference was that the final inspection called for us to wear dress uniforms.

We had spent many hours shining our shoes and brass belt buckles and hat brims in preparation for the event, so it came

CHAPTER SEVENTEEN

"First came ten soldiers carrying clubs... next the ten courtiers: these were ornamented all over with diamonds, and walked two and two, as the soldiers did."

"Platoon!....Tennn.....haw!!"

The sixty privates clicked to attention as easily and precisely and perfectly as one person alone. The hundreds of hours of standing in that position had left the group with a level of expertise that was remarkable. Not a muscle twitched. No strain or tension was detectable. They presented the viewers with a vision of motionless grace, like a multifigured sculpture carved in granite. Each figure was chiseled with care and placed in perfect harmony with the others, each unique but subordinate to the whole.

The pencils of the judges flew over the clipboards. It was an average display for a platoon in final drill.

"Le-ooft....hase!"

One smooth snap and Platoon 211 made a left face.

"Huh-red....haw!"

Sixty left feet stepped out at the same instant to start the forward march. With perfect alignment and heels digging into the asphalt we moved into a series of split second maneuvers that only the most sophisticated observer could fully appreciate. "ON-OO-EE-IDA—LEP-TWO-THREE....." The DI counted the cadence like an artist inspired to greater than normal heights of deftness. The pressure of being judged by his superiors was as no surprise to find that the inspiration was quick and efficient with no major deficiencies found or really even looked for.

When the CO came to me he inspected my rifle and my person the same way he inspected the other turds. He wasn't aware, or if he was he didn't let on, that I was fined by him for being AWOL a short time before.

The inspecting party left quietly and we changed to our usual dungaree uniforms so that we could reclean our rifles—everyone had at least one spot on his weapons that was mandatorily found by the Lieutenant—and await the decision of the judges.

Now that the final testing of the platoon was over we were in a relaxed and lighthearted frame of mind. I think all of us were savoring the accomplishment on the drill field. There was no chatter or nervousness as we sat on our buckets in the sunshine. We had won and that was that.

When Sgt. Barton came out of the duty hut we already knew what he was going to say.

"Down on your faces, you worthless bunch of pussies!"

We scrambled into the push-up position in a state of utter amazement. We couldn't possibly have lost! I felt the resentment resulting from the unfair and preposterous decision rise like vomit from my belly which physically ached with loss.

The drill instructor left us on the ground for perhaps half a minute. "Get up on your feet," he said. We jumped up and stood at attention.

"At ease. The total points that Platoon 211 has accumulated, which includes a total sweep of the drill today, is sufficient to qualify them as the honor platoon. It will be so noted by a pennant, to be attached to the platoon flag and displayed at times considered reasonable by the platoon commander." He put the slip of paper he had been reading in his pocket as we erupted.

As distasteful as I found that man to be most of the time I had no choice but to salute his genius for manipulating the emotional tones of the group. If he had done as expected and simply stated the fact that we were the winners of the prestigious honor platoon title it would have been a pleasant but bland victory. It seemed necessary to have relief and release from fear of punishment as an integral part of the process if we were to really be uplifted as a result of some accomplishment. At that moment, with a deserved triumph apparently snatched from our grasp and then rescued and returned to us, there was relief to spare. With the wisdom and integrity of the judges restored in our minds we could fully appreciate what we had done.

The DI let us smoke and talk until we simmered down. Then he came back out of the office and addressed us.

"I want to make one thing clear to you assholes before another minute goes by. Your training is by no means finished. You are still turds and will be turds until you get on the bus to leave here. There is still work to be done and one helluva lot for you screws to learn. Just because we have the necessary number of points to take honors does not mean that we are going to slack off now. Believe me, girls, there's still plenty of time to step on your dicks.

"At the same time I want you to keep in mind that this is the honor platoon of the battalion. I expect you to act like it. Those other shitbirds are gonna have their eyes on you every place you go. When you are traveling I want you to lean back and march. I want to hear your heels drown out the other platoons as we pass. You have a duty to the tradition of this holy place to be on the alert every minute of every day from now until you graduate to be the best goddam platoon on the base. The other drill instructors and I have busted our asses to get you fuckers where you are today and I have no intention of letting you fuck it up. Keep in mind that you are the elite of all the turds here and act that way.

"Tomorrow is Sunday. When we return from breakfast the smoking lamp will be lit and will stay lit all day unless you do something to douse it. You will be allowed to buy one newspaper and read it. You will be taken to the athletic field in the afternoon to play football and volleyball. In the evening you will be going to the base theatre for a movie. The other platoons will follow their normal routine.

"Don't get swelled-headed about this or you'll fuck up and I'll land all over you. Dismissed."

Incredible! We were going to have a day of actual fun! Sgt. Barton was once again, this time indelibly and forever, imprinted on our minds and in our hearts as the Forgiving Father.

CHAPTER EIGHTEEN

"Who cares for you?" said Alice (she had grown to her full size by this time). "You're nothing but a pack of cards!"

At this the whole pack rose up into the air, and came flying down upon her; she gave a little scream, half of fright and half of anger, and tried to beat them off, and found herself lying on the bank, with her head in the lap of her sister, who was gently brushing away some dead leaves that had fluttered down from the trees on to her face.

"Wake up, Alice dear!" said her sister. "Why, what a long sleep you've had!"

Graduation day started out the same as the other days had; with a snarling, bellowing drill instructor threatening the health and safety of any private who wasn't out of the rack and on the street in two minutes flat. When the lights snapped on and the noise started I had the same sinking sensation I had grown to expect upon awakening. When the recognition dawned that it was the day I had lived for, my eyelids snapped open and my mind awoke to the sensations around me. Usually I tried to block out as much as possible in the early morning, but that morning, above all mornings, I wanted to drink in every sound and smell and sight that was available to me.

I kicked off the covers and jumped to the floor. There was no time to let the pleasure of our imminent release sink in so I quickly dressed, made the rack, and ran outside.

We did the usual routine cleanup and it wasn't until we

started calisthenics that the first small bubble of joy rose from within and burst upon my consciousness. I was warm and strong and ready.

When we lined up to march to the chow hall Sgt. Liebermann said, "Get those top buttons unhooked, turds." That was all. A few little words and another bubble of happiness broke.

We started out for the mess hall and it gradually dawned on everyone in the platoon that we were home free. Even those who had thrived on the pain and humiliation and aggravation were aroused now that the end of the ordeal was at hand. The most shameless asskisser could not help but feel gladdened that he was no longer going to be cursed and threatened by the DIs. Even if accepting and enjoying what we had experienced was a private's particular way of surviving the program he had to be happy that it was over.

As the realization of the impending release took hold of the group we marched as we had never, except in final drill, marched before. The impact of our heels digging into the street bounced off the buildings and echoed back to us. The discipline and practice that was used to force us into the mold of marines was now used to proclaim that we had traveled the road and come to the end of it.

The inescapable fact was that we had survived the most rigorous and vicious treatment we would ever experience in our lifetimes barring some odd occurrence. Another fact was that the treatment had given us the capacity, both mental and physical, to kill human beings who might oppose us ideologically. The most glaring fact of all, yet the most subtle, was that we were brainwashed. This last fact could be stated more delicately and usually is, but, in layman's terms, a more accurate statement of the condition would be impossible. Some of the privates were more brainwashed than others but all were brainwashed to the degree that we dared not assess and express our true considerations on the matters that we, as soldiers, had to deal with. Few of the men in the platoon enjoyed basic training in the slightest but none of us would admit it to family and friends.

160

Few had ever known such degradation but most were ready to shout to the heavens of their pride in being a marine. None of us wanted to be maimed or killed but all were willing to proclaim publicly their desire to go to Vietnam and expose themselves to the possibility of that happening. We were all brainwashed to the point that we were willing to be marines for the time being. Some didn't like it much and a handful of us despised it but none of us was willing to express his private thoughts.

Brainwashed or not, we were over the hump and on our way out.

At the mess hall we swaggered through the chow line as all graduating platoons do, making sure that the jealous eyes of the turds behind us in training saw our open collars and starched uniforms. We wanted them to eat their hearts out every bit as much as we had when a graduating platoon strutted around in front of us.

We went back to the area and cleaned up the barracks and grounds, getting the place ready for the next occupants. We packed up all of our belongings in our duffel bags and loaded them in an empty hut by the road. We scrubbed everything in sight and by ten o'clock we were ready to change into our dress uniforms.

We primped and shined and eventually got ready for the parade that was the first part of the exercise. By that time the exhilaration of graduating that we felt in the early morning had worn off and was replaced by the same old grinding sensation that underlaid every other day.

For two hours we marched and sweated and listened to the band play. Our turn to pass in review came and we marched by the stand set up for the occasion. On the DI's command we turned our heads to the right so the general could see our faces. I was surprised to see that he looked like any normal middle-aged, middle-class person, and I took satisfaction in the knowledge that I had burgled his football equipment shack and listened to Gary Scriver getting a piece of ass on top of his team's jerseys.

We went to lunch and then back to platoon street and waited for the DI to tell us when the big moment was. At last, at long long last, it was happening. We were marching to the base theatre.

Along the way we passed several platoons in different phases of training. Some were nearly brand new, just learning how to do column turns and other basic movements in close order drill. A couple were in the latter stages of training and looked sharp while their DI put them through the paces. I saw one motley crew struggling across· the parade grounds fighting with the fartsacks who were loaded down with gear. Their faces were pictures of fear and shock, their eyes glazed over with the unreality of the introduction they had received. We had experienced everything that the other groups were then going through and so I knew how they felt. I reveled in the fact that I was not with them.

At the theatre we had to wait for everything to get set up properly. I automatically reached into my left breast pocket for the little red book, caught myself, and realized that I would never have to look at the thing again.

While we waited my mind drifted back to the many, many incidents that made up the total experience of our training. I recalled the tiredness that was deeply imbedded in my bones for the first three or four weeks and how I used to sleep on my feet when the DIs weren't watching. I remembered how my emotional responses had roller-coasted up and down violently from pure grief to rage to exhilaration. The hundreds of funny little things flashed through my mind. A lot of it wasn't real funny at the time but in retrospect much that had occurred actually deserved a laugh. I remembered my friend, Private Johnson, being hauled away in handcuffs and we thought he would go to prison for years because he skipped church. The look on John's face that day was enormously funny. Gary Scriver and his refusal to take anything seriously was a fond memory.

Most of all, standing there waiting for the ceremony to begin, I remembered the people who had handled us in the eleven weeks we were in the program. Our drill instructors, Sgts. Barton,

Liebermann, and Lofgren. The short, mean Sgt. Miller. Sgt. Torres, who would have been dead and buried if I had had a live bullet that day at the range. I remembered the classroom instructors and the other corporals and sergeants who were in charge of one thing or another. The more I recalled the more aware I became of the magnitude of the training. There were literally hundreds of people involved. I was still in a spin even though it would be finished in a matter of minutes. My memories evoked an emotional reaction that took me by surprise. The strange emotion that I felt was a cold, bitter disgust and disrespect for those who had been our captors for so long. I could not turn around and embrace a system that crushed us and then covered up the fact with mom's apple pie and dress blue uniform.

I woke up and dropped my negative thoughts as we got the command to move into the auditorium of the theatre. I was happy again. It was finally happening and I didn't want to mar the process of release with bitterness or regret.

We sat and listened as the Chaplain talked of God's plan for us and how we must accept our burdens as well as our good fortune. He told how God was on the side of democracy and righteousness and if we should be unlucky and get shot we shouldn't worry about it because the Lord knew what he was doing and we didn't. I tried to keep in mind my resolve to stay happy during the ceremony so I pictured the Chaplain not as a bad man masquerading as a messenger for the Almighty, but as a man who found it necessary to prance about the stage talking like a child. He never thought about what he was suggesting but only repeated it. The truth was, and I knew it but refused to let it ruin my day, that the Chaplain was basically an idiot who was so shallow and stupid that he couldn't differentiate between the truth and the river of lies that poured out of his fat, pampered mouth.

The Commanding General and the Battalion Commander talked. Each in his own way said the same thing. They told us of the pride inherent in being a marine, how only the very cream of America's crop of youths was allowed into the Marine Corps. They talked of toughness, honor, duty, loyalty, and the spirit that made the Marines the envy of fighting men all around the world. They touched on the subject of manhood and explained how being a marine and being a man was the same thing. A man was willing to do what men had done for hundreds of years—fight and suffer and die, willingly and nobly, for their country and their corps.

The base Sergeant-Major talked about South Vietnam and how we were saving a decent and honest democracy from the encroaching communist forces. We were not to believe the red sympathizers when they told lies about South Vietnam being a corrupt regime. The people of Vietnam needed us the way others had, almost 200 times in our history. The Marine Corps was going into the country to straighten it out and then leave. We had been fixing foreign nations up for almost two hundred years, from Cuba to China to Africa to France and never failed to make them see things our way. Vietnam was no different.

I looked around and saw the many eyes of Platoon 211. Most were shining with inspiration.

The ceremonies ended and we walked out to the parade field directly in front of the theatre. We were now offically classified as U.S. Marines. I did not find the idea of fighting for the U.S.A. hard to accept. The bullshit that went with it was a little too much but I knew in my heart that if my country actually was in danger I would defend it willingly.

Sgt. Barton and Sgt. Liebermann stood in front of the platoon as we waited for the band to start playing. They did not smile or joke or congratulate us. They merely stood in front of us with the same air of indifference and dominance that they had shown for eleven weeks.

Sgt. Barton spoke. "When you are dismissed you will be on base liberty until 1500 hours. At that time you will report back to platoon area and prepare to board the buses to Camp Pendleton. Do not leave the base for any reason and do not fill yourselves with pogey bait. Stay away from the turds who are still in training. You may go anywhere on the base that is not being used for training purposes."

"TEEEEEN-HAW!"

164

The band started playing the Marine Corps hymn and we snapped our hands to the brim of our covers in a salute.

Being part of a group with a tradition as long and proud as the U.S. Marines was sensed by us during the training and now, in our final moment of boot camp, that pride and belonging was like a long-awaited breath of air. It had been building up for weeks and the emotion swept over the group in tangible waves. We were beaming with personal and group accomplishment.

> "From the halls of Montezuma
>   to the shores of Tripoli,
> We have fought our country's battles
>   on the shore, on land and sea."

The feeling started in my toes and worked its way up my body. My stomach was warm and there was a lump in my throat.

> "First to fight for right and freedom
>   and to keep our honor clean,
> We are proud to bear the title
>   of United States Marine."

My body was strong and healthy and the blood was singing as it pounded and danced through my veins.

> "If the Army and the Navy
>   ever look on heaven's scenes,
> They will find the streets are guarded
>   by United States Marines."

I made it! The last notes of the band faded out. I won! I wanted to jump up and shout for all the world to hear that it was over and I had been set free! I was alive and alert and above all, I had fought off the programming. I would follow orders and play the game but I would not follow blindly and I would maintain to the end my right to think for myself. The majority of the privates were fully programmed and it would take anywhere from days to years to wear it off. Some never would.

Sgt. Liebermann looked at us and growled, almost resentfully, "Dismissed!"

Most of the privates were going to the enlisted men's club. I said I'd meet them later and headed for the obstacle course. When I got to a quiet area I started whistling out loud. It had been nearly three months since I had had the simple pleasure of whistling and it meant a lot to me to be able to do it just as loud as I damn well pleased.

I thought I was alone but I wasn't. From behind a quonset hut popped the familiar face of Gary Scriver.

There was a twinkle in his eyes as he asked, "Hey Danny, what's going on? You all right?"

I was glad to see him. "I'm OK, man. Just out for a little stroll."

Scriver looked around as he habitually did when he was ready to spring into action of some illegal sort. He tossed his head, indicating that I should follow him.

"Now what are you up to, Gary? The last thing I need right now is one of your plots," I said.

"No sweat," he said cheerfully and pulled up his pant leg to reveal a half pint of Old Granddad. "Just a little celebration drink to top off the day," he smiled.

"Where did you get that?" I asked, alarmed but intrigued at the idea of a good hot belt of whiskey to "top off the day."

Scriver shrugged his shoulders and we went behind the hut and took a good long pull at the bottle. It tasted terrible. It was fitting.

I told Private Scriver of the scenario that I had been day-dreaming about for the past couple of weeks and he said he would be humbled and honored if I would allow him to take part in the private graduation ceremony I had planned.

Since he was a good and loyal friend I would include him in my plan, I told him. We were dizzy but not really drunk as we made our way toward the platform used by the log exercise instructor.

166

It was quiet when we reached our destination. We climbed up on the platform and looked around at the field that had soaked up so much of our sweat. The hot wind blew on us and kicked up little dust storms in the sand where we had grunted and thrashed to exhaustion many times.

We had another snort of whiskey and I arranged it so that we could see the pole on top of the theatre that bore the flag of the honor platoon, number 211.

I said out loud what I'd rehearsed silently as my sarcastic farewell to the Marine Corps Recruit Depot. Private Gary Scriver and I stood at attention, focused on the flag.

"I salute the United States Marine Corps, I salute the drill instructors who made us into supermen, and I salute the tradition of one hundred and ninety years of blood. Above all, I salute the flag of the honor platoon, number two-eleven."

Private Scriver and I raised our arms. We stood motionless, with right fist straight out, and middle finger extended, in a salute to the making of marines.

We ended the private ceremony and climbed off the platform laughing. We shook hands to congratulate ourselves and walked on down the road.

❦   ❦   ❦

December, 1968

After an eternal wait the day finally came when the Marine Corps and I were to part company. Three years, ten months, eleven days, and six hours of service to my country left me a deeply exhausted, angry person.

I went over to a full length mirror that hung from the green plaster wall at the south end of the barracks and checked out my dress uniform for the final time. I didn't like what I saw there. I was a wreck. My knee had swollen from fever so I held my body up with the crutches that the Navy doctor had so generously issued me. ("You can go ahead and bring them home with you, marine," he had said with a smile.) The shoulder that had been carved up was still swollen and wrapped with thick bandages so that the arm fell unnaturally over the left crutch. I stepped closer to the reflection. The face seemed old and leathery. There were deep wrinkles around the eyes. The cheeks had the hollow look of the very thin. Worry lines, that looked as though a surgeon had slipped, criss-crossed the forehead. The eyes had an abnormal strength, like someone with a terminal illness who still had enough vitality to fight back. They were pin-pointed from the painkillers that had become an habitual part of my life. There was no wisdom in the eyes, only a strange, elusive quality that indicated a great capacity for endurance. I whispered a "fuck you" at the uniform in the mirror and walked away.

The room in which the Big Moment was to take place was jammed with marines itching to get released. A highway patrolman gave a recruiting pitch. A S/Sgt. gave instructions on how we were to go about picking up our pay. Nobody seemed very interested in anything except getting the papers.

Finally they lined us up and handed out the separation documents in alphabetical order. We were ushered out of the room and that was that. There were no speeches, no thank you's, no well dones. There was only the simple act of handing papers to a ragged looking group of old young men and of shooing them out the door.

I took the envelope, tucked it under my arm and swung my crutches down the concrete steps. I felt dirty. The joy and relief I had envisioned for years wasn't present, not in my heart or in the eyes of the people I had sweated and cursed and drank and killed with for so long. I had no goodbyes to make, no addresses to write down, no promises to keep. There was only a vague feeling that what I had done was wrong. I had relegated myself to the level of a beast; a mindless, soulless animal, capable of committing unspeakable violations of human dignity. I pulled the ribbons from my uniform and walked toward the green trash container parked along the side of the building. *"Oh my God, I am heartily sorry..."*
Fucking knee hurts.

168

"for having offended Thee..."
Man, I've gotta get this stuff out of my head.
"and I detest all my sins..."
We just laughed at that one family we caught after curfew, mama, papa, and baby. Blew their shit away with our '16s. Lined 'em right up and snuffed 'em. They were whining and shaking like puppies, when they realized they were going to die.
"because I dread the loss of Heaven and the pain of Hell..."
Good thing I got the bottle of percodan from the Doc. I can ease away from the shit now that I'm back in the world.
"to confess my sins, to do penance..."
At least I'm alive and more or less in one piece. I'll just spend a couple of days stoned and forget it ever happened.
Maybe I'll get a job or something.
"and to amend my life, Amen."
I know one thing—they'll never get me back in this green sonofabitch, not ever, ever again.

169

EPILOGUE

What doth it profit a man if he gains his soul but suffers the loss of the whole world?

The process of plumbing the depths of human experience is a tremendous boon to the person who does it. Once the bottom line is reached nothing can ever again destroy what is good and clean and sustaining.

On the other hand, if a person is plunged into the pit of hell and does not come back as a complete human unit, then the brush against the bottom is a terrible disaster.

For those of us who touched the outstretched hand of violent and meaningless death and escaped its grasp there was a victory of sorts. For the men and boys who were enveloped completely by the black hand there is nothing, at least insofar as their worldly identities are concerned.

But for the truly unlucky, the ones whom the LADY deserted, there is only pain and blindness and blandness and empty days and nights. There are tubes and hooks and wheels in place of hands and legs and penises. There are plastic masks over faces too ugly to be seen in public. There are weeks and months and years of waiting for nothing—of NO JOBS AND NO PRODUCTION. Would you buy a used car from someone with no face?

Of course, everybody knows a "Johnny down the block" who is making good despite his wheelchair. The trouble is that the only people we ever see are the "Johnnys" who make good. We never, ever, see the Sams and Freds who are still in the back ward at the VA hospital, getting washed and turned once a day whether they need it or not.

I can't tell you what we should do about them. The damage is already done and we can't turn a piece of smashed meat back into a human being no matter how much we want to.

I'm not banging the drum for Fred and Sam or even for Johnny. It's about fifteen years too late for that. But what I can beat the drum about is the future.

Watch the Almighty tube. Read the newspapers. Look at the billboards. See the All-Pro halfback tell your son about the wonderful opportunities available in the New Army. Look at the movie star explaining the options available and the fantastic starting pay if your boy will only sign up now. He'll get action, adventure, a chance to travel, he'll be part of the team, vocational training absolutely free, he'll see what he's made of. Watch Uncle Bob tell about Korea and how tough it was. A man's man. A chip off the old block. Bring out the Purple Heart and pass it around. Let Johnny see. Or Fred. Or Sam.

I would like to advise you to simply run the old soldiers off your property when they start their talk of glory, but that is not realistic. Your boy will still be reached by the aging ex-football heroes in the mass media.

This book was not written for the purpose of presenting a balanced view of war and its masters. If you don't agree with the viewpoint I've put forth, I'd like to make a deal with you.

I will look in awe at the pretty medals, the fine certificates, and the pictures of local homecoming parades. I will listen intently to the head of the VFW and the Generals and the industrialists and the economists. Perhaps my opinion of the Mourning Glory syndrome will be modified.

Your part of the deal is to visit your local VA hospital, find your way past the spit and polish of the easily accessible areas, and search out the invalid ward. Look around until you find an old man of about twenty-seven or twenty-eight. His name will be either Fred or Sam.

Ask him how it feels to lose the whole world.